University of
Toronto

THE CAMPUS GUIDE

University of Toronto

AN ARCHITECTURAL TOUR BY

Larry Wayne Richards

PHOTOGRAPHS BY

Tom Arban

WITH AN ESSAY BY

Martin L. Friedland

FOREWORD BY

George Baird

PRINCETON ARCHITECTURAL PRESS

NEW YORK

Published by
Princeton Architectural Press
37 East Seventh Street
New York, New York 10003

For a free catalog of books, call 1.800.722.6657.
Visit our website at www.papress.com.

Many of the buildings and architects mentioned in this book have received important honors and awards.
Although it was not possible to methodically list every honor and award, the author has referred to some of the
key ones.

Series editor: Nancy Eklund Later
Project editor and layout: Nicola Bednarek
Mapmaker: Matt Knutzen

The maps were based on imagery by © TRIATHLON LTD. 1995. Processed and distributed by Triathlon
Ltd., a subsidiary of MacDonald Dettwiler and Associates Ltd. (MDA)

Special thanks to: Nettie Aljian, Sara Bader, Dorothy Ball, Janet Behning, Becca Casbon, Carina Cha, Penny
(Yuen Pik) Chu, Russell Fernandez, Pete Fitzpatrick, Wendy Fuller, Jan Haux, Clare Jacobson, Aileen Kwun,
Nancy Eklund Later, Linda Lee, Laurie Manfra, John Myers, Katharine Myers, Lauren Nelson Packard,
Jennifer Thompson, Paul Wagner, Joseph Weston, and Deb Wood of Princeton Architectural Press
—Kevin C. Lippert, publisher

Library of Congress Cataloging-in-Publication Data
Richards, Larry Wayne.
 University of Toronto : the campus guide : an architectural tour / by Larry Wayne Richards ; photographs by
Tom Arban ; with an essay by Martin L. Friedland ; foreword by George Baird.
   p. cm.
 Includes bibliographical references and index.
 ISBN 978-1-56898-719-4 (alk. paper)
 1. University of Toronto—Buildings. I. Arban, Tom. II. Friedland, Martin L. III. Title.
LE3.T53R53 2009
378.1'9609713541—dc22

2008031583

CONTENTS

This book is intended for visitors, alumni, and students who wish to have an insider's look at the University of Toronto campuses, from Frederic Cumberland's magnificent 1859 University College, to John Andrew's megastructural Scarborough College of 1966, to Foster + Partners' exhilarating Leslie L. Dan Pharmacy Building of 2006.

The guide opens with an introduction that discusses the historical context of the institution's architecture. The architectural tour consists of nine walks covering some 170 buildings. Each building is illustrated and discussed within its architectural and social context and tied to the evolution of the university. A three-dimensional map identifies the buildings on the walk.

Visitors are welcome to tour the University of Toronto's three campuses:
St. George Campus: The Nona Macdonald Visitors Centre is located centrally on the St. George campus in the southeast corner of Knox College, 25 King's College Circle, and provides information on the university's programs, symposia, and events. The Visitors Centre features an expanded campus tour program for prospective and current students and their families, alumni, and other visitors. General walking tours are offered daily, Monday through Friday at 11 AM and 2 PM and on Saturdays and Sundays at 11 AM (holiday weekends excluded). Historical tours are offered during June, July, and August daily Monday through Friday at 10:30 AM, 1:00 PM, and 2:00 PM (holiday weekends excluded). To book a tour call (416) 978-5000.

Scarborough Campus: Tours of the Scarborough campus leave from the Admissions and Student Recruitment office in the Arts and Administration Building, near the main entrance to the campus, Monday to Thursday at 1:00 PM and Friday at 11:00 AM. A tour can be booked online at http://webapps. utsc.utoronto.ca/campus_tours/tours.php or by calling (416) 287-7529.

Mississauga Campus: Information about tours of the Mississauga campus can be found online at http://registrar.utm.utoront.ca/student/tours_ events/guided_tours.php. Tours are offered Monday to Friday in the morning and afternoon. Additional information is available at (905) 828-5400.

For more information on the University of Toronto, visit www.utoronto.ca.

FOREWORD

In his introduction to this volume, Martin Friedland names Robert Falconer (1907–32), Claude Bissell (1958–71), and Robert Prichard (1990–2000) as three presidents of the University of Toronto over its century-and-a-half-long history that stand out for their interest in its physical growth. While I did not, of course, personally experience the presidency of Falconer, I was a student at the university during the presidency of Bissell and a faculty member during that of Prichard. As a consequence, I have clear recollections of those two notable presidents.

Indeed, during my student days at the university in the early 1960s, I took it upon myself to arrange a meeting with President Bissell, on account of my dismay at an architectural decision the university had taken. The issue in question was the design of an addition to University College, one of the earliest built—and to this day, one of the most admired—buildings on the campus. The original University College is a bold essay in nineteenth-century Romanesque revival. The design for the proposed addition was a problematic mid-twentieth-century version of Romanesque revival: much paler and more timid than the original. I had recently seen photographs of some remarkable new additions at Brasenose College, Oxford. Designed by the London architecture firm Powell and Moya, they were strikingly modern and contrasted provocatively with the medieval college buildings. It was my plan—I thought of myself as a precocious young student of architecture—to persuade President Bissell that a similar approach should be taken for the addition to University College.

On the day of my appointment, President Bissell graciously welcomed me to his office, invited me to make my case, and heard me out patiently. He paused for a few moments and then responded, as best I can recall, as follows:

> Mr. Baird, you have an expert interest in architecture, and I do not. I, on the other hand, as president of this university, have charge of a considerable number of pressing files with which I am obligated to deal. For all I know, you may be right in your opinion, but I must tell you that this file is not going to be added to those in which I am already involved. In conclusion, I thank you for coming to see me to express your concern.

With that, he showed me to the door of his office. I think it was at that point that I first realized how presumptuous it had been of me to approach him in this matter and how surprising it was that he—the president of a university with, already at that time, a population of some thirty thousand students—agreed to meet with an individual undergraduate student. I was impressed by how forthright he had been with me in regard to both the substance and the political context of the issue I had raised.

Martin Friedland's and Larry Richards's commentaries have put this personal recollection of mine in a sharp new light, as they made me realize the magnitude of the transformation of the university's campuses that occurred under Bissell's leadership. The completion of the westerly expansion of the downtown St. George campus, as well as the initiation of the University of Toronto Scarborough and the University of Toronto Mississauga all occurred on his watch. Moreover, the individual buildings completed during his presidency include the two indisputable modern masterpieces at the university: Ron Thom's Massey College on the St. George campus and John Andrews's original Scarborough College building on the Scarborough campus. Bissell probably had little directly to do with the astonishing architectural quality of Massey College, since its design and construction were so closely monitored by the Massey family, its sponsors. But the original building at Scarborough College is another matter. Its design was entrusted to a team from my faculty that included the then-young John Andrews. The dramatic building that Andrews designed for Scarborough is one of the few Canadian buildings from the 1960s that rapidly attracted admiration from architects and critics around the world. Bissell must surely have assented to the bold experiment of hiring Andrews and of approving his daring design.

More recently, a commitment to quality in architectural design has become university policy. President Prichard, a true architectural enthusiast, inaugurated the university's Design Review Committee in 1997. It has the mandate to review the evolving design quality of every major new architectural project on any of the three campuses. Recent years have seen the completion of a number of impressive new architectural and landscape projects, including the redesign of St. George Street, the arterial street that divided the historic campus of the university from the western extension created in the 1960s. The triumphant redesign of this street, which includes symbolic new gates at its north and south ends, makes the former boundary between the historic east campus and the more modern west one into a new public focal space for the campus as a whole.

The university's commitment to quality architecture and landscape design continues to this day under the leadership of President David Naylor. It is a result of the institution's enlightened design policies that the University of Toronto, among its peers, clearly stands out for its handsome landscapes and its distinct and compelling architecture. Friedland and

Wilson Gate, St. George Street

Richards have truly captured the history and the essential character of this complex institution. Taking any of the varied walks described by Richards is a most rewarding urban and architectural experience.

George Baird, Dean
John H. Daniels Faculty of Architecture, Landscape, and Design
University of Toronto

W. Wesbroom, Bird's-Eye View of Toronto, *circa 1878*

The University of Toronto is a complex institution with a long history. Growing out of the federation of a number of colleges and the affiliation of many professional schools and bodies, it is today one of the largest universities in North America, with over seventy thousand students on its three campuses. Like all other major universities in Canada, it is a public university, primarily financed by the provincial government.

During the past one and a half centuries, a number of talented presidents have led the institution. Three presidents, in particular, stand out in their vision concerning the physical growth and architecture of the university: Robert Falconer (1907–32), Claude Bissell (1958–71), and Robert Prichard (1990–2000). They helped transform the University of Toronto from its small nineteenth-century beginnings as a successor of Toronto's first institute of higher learning, King's College, into today's hugely successful university with three campuses in and near the city of Toronto.

King's College

On March 15, 1827, the Crown in England issued a charter to John Strachan, an Anglican minister, to establish a college in Upper Canada, now the province of Ontario, "for the education of youth in the principles of the Christian Religion, and for their instruction in the various branches of Science and Literature." The college, called King's College, was to be at or near the town of York, now the city of Toronto. Strachan, who would become the college's first president, wanted such an institution, he wrote, to avoid sending students for their education to the United States, where "the school books... are stuffed with praises of their own institutions, and breathe hatred to everything English."

The council of the college purchased a site consisting of 150 acres of vacant forest land north of the town of York—today downtown Toronto—from three owners at a price of £3,750, a sum about equal to the cost of Strachan's fine home on Front Street, overlooking Lake Ontario. In 1829 the eminent English architect Charles Fowler, who was then designing London's Covent Garden Market, completed drawings for the new college and sent a model showing a Greek-revival design resembling Thomas Jefferson's University of Virginia to Upper Canada. While some of the land was cleared and title to a grand avenue (now University Avenue) leading from Queen Street to the site where the legislative buildings of Ontario now stand was purchased, Fowler's design was never built.

Many people in Upper Canada strongly objected to the fact that the college would accept only members of the Church of England, and the

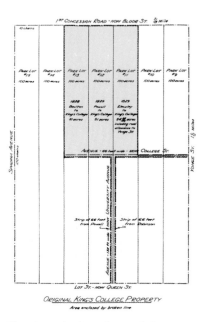

Plan, drawn in the early twentieth century,
showing the original 150-acre property
obtained by King's College in 1828, plus
the university-owned roads that became
University Avenue and College Street

Upper Canada legislative assembly proceeded to condemn the charter—a position that the British House of Commons strongly endorsed. In response, the council of the college, with the approval of the colony's legislative assembly, made some changes: professors, for example, no longer had to be members of the Church of England, although they had to subscribe to the doctrine of the Holy Trinity.

In 1838 Toronto architect Thomas Young, who was in the process of designing St. James Cathedral on King Street after one of the city's fires, completed new plans for King's College. Young's classical design envisioned three buildings: a center block containing the library, a convocation hall, and a museum, with classrooms in the west block and a residence in the east block. All three would be connected by a covered walkway. Only the residence was built—completed in 1843—but it was torn down in 1886 to make way for the present legislative buildings in Queen's Park. Classes were held in a vacant building on Front Street.

Creation of the University of Toronto

On January 1, 1850, the Parliament of Canada passed a law to secularize King's College, which was to be replaced by a new university that was not connected with the Church of England anymore. The University of Toronto, as the new institution was called, took over the charter and the land and buildings of its predecessor. Strachan denounced the "godless" institution and went on to create a new Anglican college, Trinity College, which was located on the site of the present Trinity-Bellwoods Park, on Queen Street West. Trinity College would eventually join the University of Toronto in 1904.

Many members of the staff of King's College continued at the University of Toronto, including the president of King's, John McCaul. Only about fifty full-time students attended the new institution in the 1850s—roughly the same number as had been at King's College. In order to increase

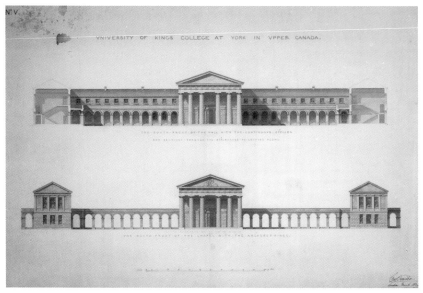

South elevations of Charles Fowler's 1829 Greek-revival design for the University of King's College at York in Upper Canada

enrollment, President McCaul and others proposed a reorganization of the university that would give an incentive to other colleges, such as the various denominational colleges in Upper Canada, including the Presbyterian Queen's College in Kingston, the Methodist Victoria College in Cobourg, and the Roman Catholic Regiopolis College in Kingston, to affiliate with it. The University of Toronto Act was amended in 1853 to give these other colleges representation on the university senate. The new model was based on that of the University of London: University College became a nonreligious arts and science teaching college, while the university itself, like the University of London, became an examining body.

University College was able to hire a credible group of professors. Toronto was now a wealthy city of about forty thousand people and was growing rapidly. Daniel Wilson from Scotland, appointed as the professor of British history and literature and later succeeding McCaul as president, wrote to his wife shortly after he arrived in 1853 about his first impressions:

> It is a busy, bustling, active town…bearing such evident marks of rapid increase that I should not wonder if ten years hence it be found to number nearer a hundred thousand.…Everything indicates wealth and prosperity. As to the shops, many of them are equal to the best in Edinburgh, and if a person has only money, he need want for nothing here that he desires.

William Storm, architectural rendering of "Toronto University" [University College], circa 1857

Not all the appointments were as good as that of Wilson. Sometimes politics played an undue role: the great Thomas Huxley was an applicant for a science chair and came recommended by the leading scientists in England, including Charles Darwin. The government, however, decided to appoint the undistinguished Reverend William Hincks, who just happened to be the brother of the premier.

The first college to become associated with the University of Toronto was Knox College, a Presbyterian divinity school that had broken away from the official Church of Scotland; others would not join until several decades later. In 1875 Knox College opened a distinctive, churchlike structure in the middle of Spadina Avenue, north of College Street, which still stands and now houses part of the art department. It appears prominently in a circle at the upper left in a circa 1878 bird's-eye-view engraving of Toronto (see page 10).

Constructing University College

During the first few years of its existence, University College had to use temporary facilities to teach its students, because the government wanted the site of the former King's College building at the top of University Avenue for a legislative building. Not only did University College need a proper home, the university also wanted to use some of its original endowment on a new building before the denominational colleges, which were now represented on the university senate, could get their hands on it. "Every stone that goes up in the building, every book that is bought," wrote the vice-chancellor at the time, "is so much more anchorage, and so much less plunder to fight for." The cornerstone for the magnificent University College building was laid in 1856, and the capstone for its 120-foot tower was set in place in 1858. Most people would agree that University College, designed by Frederic Cumberland, one of Canada's greatest architects of the nineteenth century, is the University of Toronto's finest historic building. Within a relatively brief period of time after arriving in Canada in 1847 at the age of twenty-seven, Cumberland had been involved in important projects, including St. James's Cathedral and the Adelaide Street courthouse. While working on University College, the architect was also busy with the equally fine expansion of Osgoode Hall. When Anthony Trollope visited Toronto in 1862, he wrote that "the two sights of Toronto" were Osgoode Hall and University College, the latter of which he called "the glory of Toronto." The two buildings are prominent in the circa 1878 bird's-eye-view engraving, in which University College appears amidst forested green and Osgoode Hall can be found at the south end of University Avenue. Almost all of Cumberland's buildings survive today, including his residence, Cumberland House, completed in 1860 on the east side of St. George Street, just north of College Street, and now the International Student Centre. Even the government's Magnetic and Meteorological Observatory building (previously the Royal Magnetical Observatory) by Cumberland, constructed in the early 1850s, still survives, although in a somewhat different form. Its stones were used to construct the observatory just east of University College, a building that now houses the Students' Union organization.

At first, Cumberland and his partner, William Storm, designed a Gothic structure for University College, but the Governor General, who wanted an Italian-looking building, was unhappy with the design. They then considered a Byzantine style. In the Governor General's absence, however, they redesigned the building once again. The vice-chancellor of the university wrote:

> We polished away almost all traces of Byzantine and got a hybrid with some features of Norman, of early English etc. with faint traces of Byzantium and the Italian palazzo, but altogether a not unsightly building.

As Cumberland once explained, he chose the Norman Romanesque style because he "believed that its ruggedness was appropriate to Canada." The architect had been influenced by John Ruskin, the nineteenth-century English art and social critic, who, using the example of English castles, urged young architects "to conceive and deal with breadth and solidity" and stressed the importance of craftsmanship—all features that are found in University College.

Lucius O'Brien, watercolor of McCaul's Pond with University College in the background, 1876

An imposing structure, the main front of the south-facing building is nearly four hundred feet long and could then be seen from the city and the lake. East of University College was Taddle Creek, a stream that ran from Wychwood Park on the high ground north of what was then the city, along the present Philosopher's Walk and past University College, making its way to Lake Ontario. In 1859 a dam was built just east of University College, to form a pond known over the years as McCaul's Pond. The creek appears and reappears in the history of the university. It was covered over in 1884 and made a city sewer, having become, as noted by a local newspaper at the time, "a holding tank for all the sewage discharged into Taddle Creek by residents of Yorkville upstream." Even after it was buried, the creek's existence has played a role in the location and design of other buildings, including Hart House to the east of University College and Mount Sinai Hospital on University Avenue, because of concerns with foundations and drainage.

The west wing of University College was a men's residence. President Daniel Wilson (1880–92) advocated for a separate college for women, but the Ontario government preferred coeducational classes, and so in 1884 the first female students officially attended lectures at University College. The college did not provide residences for women, however, and they were forced to find lodgings in boarding houses. The first University College residence for women, using a home on Queen's Park Circle, since torn down, was not opened until 1905. A larger women's residence, Whitney Hall (now coeducational), was built in 1931.

View from the southwest of Saint Basil's Church and College of Saint Michael, Toronto *as proposed by architect William Hay in 1855*

Other Colleges

In the 1880s, the university made another attempt to induce the denominational colleges to join. The Roman Catholic St. Michael's College, founded in 1852 and at the time primarily a theological college, affiliated with the university in 1881. A vision of what the college and its church, St. Basil's, might be on Clover Hill—a tight cluster of Gothic-inspired structures—was presented by architect William Hay in 1855. A simpler version of the ensemble officially opened in 1856 on Clover Hill, the highest piece of land on the downtown campus, and St. Basil's Church and the adjacent Odette Hall remain as the university's oldest surviving buildings. After World War One, St. Michael's developed more ambitious plans, with the establishment of the world-renowned Pontifical Institute of Mediaeval Studies on Queen's Park Crescent East.

The Presbyterian Knox College continued its affiliation with the university, as did Wycliffe College, which had been founded in 1877 by Low Church Anglicans who wanted "to combat the Catholic heresies allegedly promoted by Trinity," and joined the university in 1885. In 1891 Wycliffe

Victoria College, looking northeast, about 1900

moved to its present location on Hoskin Avenue. Both colleges offer only divinity degrees.

In 1890, after much debate following the passage of the Federation Act of 1887, Victoria University in Cobourg, Ontario decided to federate with the University of Toronto, and the formal opening of the new Victoria College building took place two years later. William Storm, who had worked with Cumberland on the University College building, produced an impressive Romanesque-revival structure, borrowing heavily from the American architect Henry Hobson Richardson in the use of arches, colored bands, and cast-iron structural skeleton and staircases. The "Old Vic" building, as it is known, with its red sandstone and gray limestone, looks south to the new Legislative Building, which had been completed earlier that year.

Trinity College officially joined the University of Toronto in 1904, after its medical school had merged with the university's medical school the previous year. For Trinity, as for Victoria, the growing cost of science and research was a main factor in the decision to join the University of Toronto. Trinity received its present site in 1909, but did not physically move until after World War One. In 1923 the foundation stone of the current building was laid. (In fact, two foundation stones were laid, one on top of the other, because a month before the event the original foundation stone from the college's old building on Queen Street was discovered. The two stones can be seen today to the left of the main entrance.) Architects Darling & Pearson, who had been responsible for most of the major buildings on the university's campus over the previous twenty years, designed a Gothic building to resemble the old college. The present chapel, the last major work designed by the great English architect Sir Giles Gilbert Scott, was completed in 1955.

The denominational colleges were free to determine their own styles of architecture and to choose their own architects. As a result, the University of Toronto, unlike many other universities, did not have a uniform style even in its early days. Gothic, Romanesque, classical, modernist, and other designs exist side by side, enlivening the campus and making it invitingly diverse.

From the university's beginnings, the teaching of science has played a large role. The institution's first science laboratory was in University College. The round building at the college's west end, now called the Croft Chapter House, served as Professor Henry Croft's (1843–80) chemistry laboratory. One can still see the ventilation openings at the top of the structure. In the 1890s, a larger chemistry building—since demolished—was constructed at the south end of the campus. The chemistry department remained there until it moved to its present location on St. George Street in the 1960s. Known as the Lash Miller Chemical Laboratories, the new chemistry building was named after a long-serving chair of the department who, surprisingly, refused to believe in atomic theory.

A physics laboratory took chemistry's place in University College's round house, but the space was clearly inadequate, and in 1907 Darling & Pearson designed a new physics building, later called the Sandford Fleming Building, just north of the old chemistry building. The space is now occupied by the engineering department, and a new physics building, named after the professor of physics John McLennan, is located just south of the Lash Miller Chemical Laboratories.

The physics department long lobbied for a proper astronomy facility—a story that has taken many twists and turns. In 1908 the federal government's Magnetic and Meteorological Observatory at the south end of the campus was taken down as a response to several problems: the smoke in the city made it difficult to see the heavens, the new streetcar line on College Street interfered with magnetic readings, and the building's location made it difficult to create a straight entrance route into the university from the south. Although parts of the old observatory were reconstructed east of University College and served astronomy for a few decades, it was not until 1935 that a sophisticated facility—the new David Dunlap Observatory in Richmond Hill, north of Toronto—was finally built. At the time, it contained the second largest telescope in the world. In 2008, the university sold the David Dunlap Observatory and the surrounding almost two hundred acres to a developer who will keep the 1935 building intact and preserve the historic telescope. The proceeds from the sale will be invested in a newly created Dunlap Institute for Astronomy and Astrophysics.

The biology department was originally housed in a structure on Queen's Park Crescent, which officially opened in 1889. It was demolished in 1966 to make way for the Medical Sciences Building. A new zoology building, named after Professor Ramsay Wright, who had been responsible for the 1889 building, then moved to its current site on the southwest corner of St. George and Harbord streets. The botany department had earlier split off from zoology and at first occupied one of the former private residences around Queen's Park Crescent and later a building (now the Tanz Neuroscience Building) on Queen's Park Crescent West, constructed in the 1930s. Today it is housed in the Earth Sciences Centre on Willcocks Street. Its lovely greenhouses at the corner of College Street and Queen's Park were relocated in 2004 to a city park, Allan Gardens, to make room for the Leslie L. Dan Pharmacy Building.

Professional Faculties

Although King's College had had professional faculties, such as law and medicine, the University of Toronto shut them down in 1853. It continued, however, to examine candidates and offer degrees. The Federation Act of 1887 brought both law and medicine back as teaching faculties, although it was not until 1957 that the law school was fully recognized by the Law Society of Upper Canada.

After years in old houses on St. George Street, including Cumberland House, and at Glendon Hall, an estate in the north end of Toronto (now part of York University), the law school's present home consists of Sir Joseph Flavelle's splendid mansion on Queen's Park, just south of the Royal Ontario Museum, and Edward R. Wood's fine residence beside the museum, now named Falconer Hall after university president Robert Falconer.

The Faculty of Medicine was re-established in 1887, its staff consisting of doctors from the private Toronto School of Medicine, which was situated a few miles away from the university, near the Don River. In 1903 a new medical school building opened on the site of the present Medical Sciences Building, built in the late 1960s.

Following the example of Johns Hopkins University, the University of Toronto made plans for a university-owned hospital on the campus. There was, however, strong and effective objection from residents near the proposed hospital on College Street at the top of McCaul Street. In 1913 the Toronto General Hospital, originally located in the present Regent Park, near the Don River, moved to a site on the south side of College Street, east of University Avenue, and served as a teaching hospital. That original structure is now part of the recently developed MaRS Centre, designed to bring basic sciences and entrepreneurs together, with which the university is affiliated.

A large number of other professional schools became associated with the University of Toronto in the 1880s and later decades. The Royal College of Dental Surgeons of Ontario, which had been running its own school since 1875, affiliated with the university in 1888. In the late 1890s, the dentistry division opened a school on the south side of College Street, east of University Avenue. The site was, however, needed for the new Toronto General Hospital, and in 1909 a five-story building on the northeast corner of College and Huron streets—designed by Edmund Burke, who would later design the Bloor Viaduct—opened for students. Dentistry stayed there until 1959, when it moved to a new International Style building on Elm Street, north of Dundas Street.

The architecture division, which had grown out of the Faculty of Applied Science and Engineering, then took over the former School of Dentistry building in 1961 (and is still there). The university had established the department as Canada's first architectural program in 1890, and it later gained its independence from engineering. Its premises on College Street have been imaginatively renovated and include an exhibition gallery named after Eric Arthur, a highly respected professor of architecture who did much to enhance and preserve Canada's architectural heritage while simultaneously promoting modernism.

Pharmacy followed much the same pattern as dentistry. The Ontario College of Pharmacy affiliated with the university in the early 1890s, but did not physically move from its site east of Yonge Street to the campus until 1963. Its new home, the Leslie L. Dan Pharmacy Building, designed by Foster + Partners, recently opened at the northwest corner of College Street and University Avenue.

The Faculty of Applied Science and Engineering was established in 1873 as the School of Practical Science. A three-story red brick building, which was torn down in the 1960s to permit the construction of the Medical Sciences Building, opened in 1878 on King's College Circle, and the school formally affiliated with the University of Toronto in 1889. In 1904 another engineering building, the Mining Building, was constructed on the north side of College Street, and over the next century the faculty's expansion, with its many divisions, rivaled that of the Faculty of Medicine.

Later, other professional schools were established, including a Faculty of Education (1906), School of Forestry (1907), and a School of Nursing (1933), all of which originally had purpose-built, stand-alone facilities but which are now, for the most part, absorbed into the general architectural fabric of the campus.

King's College Circle

By the early years of the twentieth century, King's College Circle was increasingly ringed with buildings, with University College to the north, the School of Practical Science to the southeast, the library and the medical school

Robert Falconer (left) crossing the Front Campus lawn, near the library, on the occasion of his installation as president of the university, 1907

to the east, and Knox College, which had moved from Spadina Circle in 1915, to the west. An important addition to the east side of the circle had been the new university library, which was fully in operation in 1893. A new library had become necessary because of a devastating fire in University College in 1890—caused by a careless worker carrying kerosene lamps up a wooden staircase— which destroyed the entire collection of about thirty thousand books. The new library building, designed by David B. Dick and generally shaped like a medieval church, was isolated from other structures to prevent fires from spreading and was constructed with noncombustible material. The stacks were made of cast iron and the floors of massive sections of glass, which allowed light to penetrate from floor to floor. The architect copied the front doorway from a twelfth-century Scottish abbey that President Wilson had described in one of his early books. By 1910 a five-story glass-floored expansion into the ravine to the east was completed. The building, which was the second largest library in Canada after the Parliamentary Library in Ottawa, served the university until after World War Two.

When University College was rebuilt after the 1890 fire, it did not include a convocation hall, and convocations were temporarily held in such venues as the gymnasium and the examination hall of the School of Practical Science. Eventually, with the support of the alumni and the government, the university built the present Convocation Hall at the southwest portion of King's College Circle. Designed by Darling & Pearson, who had just completed the residence for the businessman Joseph Flavelle in Queen's Park, it was modeled on the Sorbonne theatre in Paris and was intended to seat two thousand people. The building was completed in 1906, in time for President Falconer's 1907 inauguration ceremony.

In 1923 a striking new administration building was attached to Convocation Hall—the present Simcoe Hall—further enclosing and giving definition to King's College Circle.

Compared to most other universities, the University of Toronto provided relatively few student residences in its early days. The majority of its students were from the Toronto area and lived at home. Moreover, the University College residence was closed at the end of the nineteenth century because the space was needed for teaching purposes. The university encouraged fraternities in those early years, some of which still survive around the campus, but most students lived at home or in boarding houses. In 1907 the university planned a residence quadrangle at the corner of Devonshire Place and Hoskin Avenue. Due to funding problems, only three wings of the residence, which now houses an international studies center as well as the Trinity College library, were completed.

The various affiliated colleges added residences over the years. Victoria College opened Annesley Hall, a residence for women, on Queen's Park near Bloor Street in 1903. Trinity College opened St. Hilda's College on Devonshire Place in 1939. St. Joseph's College, which occupied the grand home formerly owned by the Christie family (of Christie's biscuit fame) at the corner of Wellesley Street and Queen's Park Crescent, affiliated with St. Michael's College in 1912. A number of men's residences were built, including Victoria's Burwash Hall and St. Michael's Teefy Hall, both designed in the collegiate Gothic style.

One of the university's greatest benefactors has been the Massey family, who made their fortune in farm equipment. The Masseys were intensely interested in architecture and helped bring about Annesley Hall, Burwash Hall, and the Household Science Building (at the southeast corner of Bloor Street and Avenue Road), and in the early 1960s contributed Massey College for graduate students. Their greatest gift, however, was Hart House, a student center for men, which was not fully opened to women until 1972. It is unique in combining athletic facilities with space for music, art, debating, and many other activities. Construction of Hart House started before World War One, and it was used for training soldiers during the war. Designed by Toronto architects Sproatt & Rolph, who had been responsible for Victoria's Burwash Hall and Residences, the collegiate Gothic building officially opened in 1919. The firm of Sproatt & Rolph was awarded the American Institute of Architects prestigious Gold Medal in 1925 in recognition of their expertise in collegiate Gothic architecture. A 1925 *Toronto Star* article said, "All good architects aim to beautify cities. Sproatt eats and drinks architectural beauty."

Female students would not get suitable athletic facilities until the Clara Benson Building, designed by Fleury, Arthur & Barclay, was

Dedication of the Soldiers' Tower, 1924

constructed on the west campus in 1959. Additional athletic facilities for men and women went up to the west of the Benson Building in the 1970s. In the 1980s, many student services, such as the housing service and the bookstore, were incorporated into the Koffler Student Services Centre, the former beaux arts–inspired reference library at the northwest corner of College and St. George streets.

The university's first stadium, Varsity Stadium, was created in 1911, evolving from a cinder track and five-hundred-seat grandstand constructed south of Bloor Street in 1901, and continued to expand during the next four decades. By 1950 an average of over twenty-five thousand people would attend intercollegiate football games. The university recently demolished the stadium and replaced it with a state-of-the-art facility that seats only about five thousand spectators. An ice arena, built in 1926 just east of the stadium, seats four thousand, perhaps reflecting the relative popularity of ice hockey over field sports at the University of Toronto.

The 1920s and 1930s

After the devastating World War One, in which so many students, staff, and alumni lost their lives, the 1920s were good years for the University of Toronto. On the first anniversary of the armistice, the cornerstone for a memorial tower was laid between Hart House and University College. The magnificent bell tower, designed by the architects of Hart House, Sproatt & Rolph, was completed in 1924.

Under President Falconer's strong leadership, the university constructed a number of buildings, including the splendid Electrical Building (now the Rosebrugh Building) fronting on Taddle Creek Road (designed by Darling & Pearson). But two events at the institution in 1922 had a particularly profound effect and indirectly led to new structures. The first was Frederick Banting and Charles Best's discovery of insulin in 1922, with the subsequent awarding of the Nobel Prize for medicine jointly to Banting and to the head of the department of physiology, J. J. McLeod. Research money poured into the university, resulting, for example, in a new research institute for Banting

East facade of the Electrical (now Rosebrugh) Building, facing Taddle Creek Road, 1920s

on College Street opposite Toronto General Hospital. Insulin helped put the University of Toronto on the medical map.

The other event was the creation of the School of Graduate Studies, which helped increase enrollment of graduate students. Up until then, the number of doctoral students at the university had been very low, even though the doctorate degree had been available since 1897. The School of Graduate Studies has had various homes on the campus and is presently in two historic houses on the east side of St. George Street, 63 and 65 St. George Street, the former being the nineteenth-century home of Canada's first prime minister, Sir John A. Macdonald. The new Pontifical Institute of Mediaeval Studies at St. Michael's College also attracted graduate students, resulting in a building for the institute on the east side of Queen's Park Crescent. Similarly, the red brick and stone Rockefeller-funded School of Hygiene, which drew many foreign graduate students, was constructed on College Street, near University Avenue, in 1927.

President Falconer's successful twenty-five-year term of office ended in 1932, and the chairman of the board of governors, Canon Henry Cody, became president. It was difficult to be a creative president during the Depression, when the government was cutting its expenditures. Some construction took place, however.

The principal addition to the university in the 1930s was the expansion of the Royal Ontario Museum, which was an integral part of the University of Toronto until it formally separated for financial reasons in the 1960s. In 1914 the west wing of the museum—a three-story Byzantine-style building

Royal Ontario Museum,
University of Toronto

Postcard showing the Royal Ontario Museum, opened in 1914

designed by Darling & Pearson—had opened beside Philosopher's Walk. Using construction as an opportunity to create jobs during the Depression, the building was expanded in 1933 to three times its capacity with a handsome new wing and an entrance on Queen's Park.

World War Two and Its Aftermath

During World War Two, enrollment decreased from about eight thousand students to roughly seven thousand, although the number of engineering students actually increased. There was very little change in the physical structure of the university, although there was considerable war-related work within the institution. One result of the war was that Canada drew closer to the United States, and the link to British universities weakened. This would promote the flow of graduate students to the United States and result in the shaping of the University of Toronto's own graduate programs along American lines.

After the war, enrollment soared as Toronto took about a quarter of all the Canadian veterans who went on to university. In the academic year of 1946 to 1947, there were over seventeen thousand students, about half of them veterans. At the same time, the number of female students at the university declined from almost 50 percent of the student body to a little over 25 percent, as many women stayed home, got married, and had children. This, of course, largely accounted for the arrival of the baby boomers at universities twenty years later.

Due to the increased student numbers, the engineering department, which then included architecture, needed more space. Temporarily, it moved into the federal government's large former munitions plant in Ajax, about twenty-five miles (forty kilometers) east of Toronto. The federal government offered to give the land permanently to the university. "It seems to me," wrote Reconstruction Minister C. D. Howe, "that you will be driven out of the city eventually, and I doubt if there is any more suitable location than the one you have [at Ajax]." Fortunately, the university declined the government's offer and eventually built new engineering facilities on the Toronto campus, including the Mechanical Engineering Building on King's College Road and the Wallberg Memorial Building for chemical engineering on College Street, as well as new facilities for the Institute of Aerophysics in the north end of the city. Architecture also returned from Ajax to the main campus and was temporarily housed in the old skating arena on Huron Street.

Baby Boomers

By 1950 almost all the veterans had graduated, and overcrowding was no longer a serious problem. The economy was strong, there was relatively little unemployment, and yet the university constructed only a few buildings during that decade—a short-lived lull in construction that would end in the 1960s.

By 1955, under President Sidney Smith (1945–57), it had become clear that the baby boomers would hit the universities in the 1960s. Experts predicted that enrollment in Canada would at least double and that the numbers of students seeking to attend the University of Toronto would be disproportionately higher. A 1956 internal university report, created by the university senate's Plateau Committee, set the stage for future planning: the university should be prepared to double its enrollment; residences should be expanded; and new colleges, both downtown and on the outskirts of the metropolitan area, should be established.

It was evident that the Toronto campus would have to expand, but in what direction? An earlier 1949 report by a committee headed by Professor Eric Arthur of the School of Architecture had agreed with a still earlier 1947 report by architect and planner James Murray that the downtown campus should expand to the west. Murray had concluded that it should not extend north because of the "serious barrier of heavily traveled Bloor Street," coupled with the expense of purchasing properties in the area to the north. Murray's guiding principle was that it should take no longer than ten

Aerial view of the St. George campus looking north, 1950

minutes—the time allowed between lectures—to walk from one part of the campus to another. (It takes about ten minutes to walk from Bloor to College Street.) "A circle with its centre just south of Hart House and a diameter stretching from College Street to Bloor Street," Murray noted, "extends... west as far as Spadina."

The campus, the Plateau Committee concluded, should therefore extend west to Spadina Avenue. Up until then, the university, with a few exceptions such as the dentistry, nursing, and education divisions, did not extend west of St. George Street. In the late 1950s, the University of Toronto started quietly buying properties in that area and eventually expropriated numerous properties west of St. George Street between Bloor and College streets.

Planning for Expansion

The board of governors set up an advisory planning committee, which produced a comprehensive plan for the new thirty-three-acre campus south of Harbord Street and extending to Spadina Avenue: The campus would be reserved for pedestrian use only. Deliveries would take place via underground routes from the main city streets, and parking would be confined to lots on Spadina Avenue, which would provide a buffer from the then-contemplated Spadina Expressway. (As it turned out, the expressway was never built,

Neil McKinnon (center), member of the board of governors, with Vince Kelly (left), president, and Adrienne Poy (right), vice-president, of the Students' Administrative Council, examining a model of the west campus expansion in the late 1950s

primarily because of the opposition inspired by Jane Jacobs, who had recently moved to Toronto from New York City, only to find her own home in the path of the proposed expressway.) Moreover, the plan also provided for two large playing fields in the middle of the west campus, between the residences and athletic buildings on the west and the academic buildings on or close to St. George Street. The Faculty of Arts and Science and some other divisions were to move to the new west campus.

The planning committee also made detailed proposals for the university as a whole, most of which were later implemented under Claude Bissell's presidency, which commenced in 1958. It was a veritable building boom: University College received a new north wing in 1964, which completed the quadrangle; a centrally located arts building named after former president Sidney Smith was opened on the west side of St. George Street in 1961; the Ramsay Wright Zoological Laboratories, the Lash Miller Chemical Laboratories, and the McLennan Physical Laboratories with its Burton Tower started to appear on the west campus; and the Galbraith Building for engineering, named after the first dean of engineering, was constructed in the 1960s on the east side of St. George Street. A University of Toronto fundraising campaign had brought in $15 million, higher than its original target. Unfortunately, the government would not provide the necessary additional funding to meet the cost of the west campus expansion and the new construction, which had risen from an estimated $12 million to over $50 million, not including the cost of the land and projects already in progress.

The government was faced with additional demands from other Ontario universities, such as McMaster, which was now eligible for funding, and newly created universities, such as Carleton and Waterloo. In the summer of 1957, the chair of the university's board of governors, Eric Phillips, wrote to President Smith that although he was "much in sympathy" with the closing of the roads and the construction of two playing fields, his feeling was that "no such luxury will be accepted by the Government." These, of course, were the two crucial aspects of the west campus expansion plan. "It is my feeling," Phillips wrote, "that the layout as a whole should be based on the complete absence of playing fields from this area, and that such open space as is involved in the overall plan should be limited to what I call 'quad-rangles.'" The plan was thereafter effectively emasculated. New buildings were constructed using the existing street pattern, cars were not excluded, and there were no playing fields. This would have long-term consequences for the university.

A Flurry of Buildings

At no period in the university's history did so much construction take place in so short a time as in the 1960s. In addition to the buildings mentioned above, there were new buildings at the denominational colleges, such as the new John Kelly Library and Loretto College women's residence at St. Michael's; the new Margaret Addison Hall for Victoria College; and the Gerald Larkin Academic Building on Devonshire Place, for Trinity College.

The university also constructed new professional buildings, such as the massive concrete Medical Sciences Building on the site of the old engineering building on King's College Circle and the previously mentioned Galbraith Building. The law school moved from the Glendon estate to occupy Flavelle House, with a library and moot court room built behind it. The Faculty of Music opened a building overlooking Philosopher's Walk with two large concert halls, and the Royal Conservatory of Music (at the time closely associated with the university) took over the building that had once housed McMaster University.

As had been recommended by the Plateau Committee, the university also established two new colleges on the west campus. In 1964 the cornerstone of the first phase of a new undergraduate college—appropriately called New College—was laid at the corner of Willcocks and Huron streets. It was, as President Bissell said at the ceremony, "a new chapter in the history of the University of Toronto." It would be the first college directly under the control of the university constructed since University College was built in the 1850s. Innis College, named after political economist Harold Innis, admitted its first students in 1964, but the sod was not turned for the building at the corner of St. George and Sussex streets until 1973. Unlike New College, it did not initially have a residence, until one was built across the road on the east side of St. George Street in the 1990s.

Scarborough, 1974

Founding of Scarborough and Mississauga

Even the creation of New and Innis colleges, as well as the establishment of York University (which first admitted students in 1960 and was affiliated with the University of Toronto until 1965), would not be able to satisfy the expected demand for university places in the Toronto region. The University of Toronto therefore founded two new colleges on the outskirts of Toronto. With the encouragement of the Ontario government, it purchased two large blocks of land—a 200-acre site in Scarborough about twenty miles (thirty kilometers) east of the main campus, and a 150-acre site on the Credit River in Mississauga, the same distance west of the campus. The two new colleges, now known as University of Toronto Scarborough (UTS) and University of Toronto Mississauga (UTM), were to be like other colleges in the Toronto system, though it was envisioned that they would gradually achieve greater autonomy.

Three members of the School of Architecture, John Andrews, Michael Hough, and Michael Hugo-Brunt, worked together to plan the Scarborough site and design a building. Australian architect (and a University of Toronto professor at the time) John Andrews's imposing concrete megastructure, built in 1964, sits dramatically on a ridge overlooking the heavily wooded valley of Highland Creek below (see page 194). The *Architectural Forum* gave it a rave review, stating that "the visitor succumbs most willingly to the sheer power of the whole, to Andrews' ingenious blending of light, form and space into a single experience." Not everyone was thrilled, however. Some members of the board regarded it as "conspicuous waste."

Erindale College, 1971

Mississauga started life with a preliminary building, known today as the North Building, to greet the first class that started in 1967. Meanwhile, John Andrews developed the initial site plan and architectural vision for the campus, then known as Erindale College. Somewhat similar to Scarborough, he proposed a megastructure, which was developed further by the engineering firm of A. D. Margison and Associates in 1968 but lacked the design finesse characteristic of Andrews (see page 214). Certain aspects of the megastructure concept were given form in the pleasant South Building, designed by Raymond Moriyama in association with A. D. Margison and Associates and opened in 1971.

By the end of the 1980s, each of the two colleges was approaching some four thousand full-time students, poised to increase their size and range of activities.

Graduate Studies

The growth in the number of students attending postsecondary institutions meant that universities required more teachers, and therefore more graduate programs to produce those teachers. The University of Toronto played a major role in this endeavor. To handle the increase in graduate enrollment in engineering, for example, the university doubled the number of engineering faculty members during the 1960s. The engineering depart-ment took over the Sandford Fleming Building on King's College Road, which became physically linked to the new Galbraith Building on St. George Street.

Medicine also greatly increased its number of postgraduate students. The Medical Sciences Building was ready for use by the end of the 1960s. The Faculty of Medicine also acquired from the federal government the former veterans' hospital, Sunnybrook Hospital, in the northeast part of the city. Other affiliated teaching hospitals expanded. On University Avenue alone, there were large additions to the Hospital for Sick Children and the Toronto General Hospital. Mount Sinai Hospital built a wholly new struc-ture, because the presence of Taddle Creek did not permit additional stories on its existing building. Princess Margaret Hospital and the Ontario Cancer Institute expanded at their old site on Sherbourne Street, both later taking over one of the Hydro Buildings on University Avenue in the 1990s. (A list of hospitals and centers affiliated with the health sciences at University of Toronto is included on page 176.)

At the same time, research grew in importance at the university. The new Ontario Institute for Studies in Education (OISE), which was estab-lished in 1965 by the Ontario government and became part of the University of Toronto, had the largest number of graduate students. In 1969 it moved into its present twelve-story building on the north side of Bloor Street, con-structed specifically for OISE. Other centers and institutes followed, such as the Centre for Mediaeval Studies and the Marshall McLuhan Centre for Culture and Technology.

In the early 1960s, a final great gift by Vincent Massey enabled the establishment of a graduate college. Massey College opened in 1963 at the corner of Devonshire Place and Hoskin Avenue. Massey's son, the archi-tect Hart Massey, wanted a modern treatment; Vincent Massey, however, according to Claude Bissell, was "determinedly traditionalist." The Frank Lloyd Wright–inspired Vancouver architect Ron Thom managed to satisfy both father and son while creating a universally acclaimed building. Massey College has the feel of a traditional English college, with its inner courtyard and grand dining hall, but is also strikingly modern in design.

With the increased number of graduate students, the university needed more graduate residences, and as a result acquired two apartment buildings on Charles Street West for family housing, and a low-rise apartment build-ing at the southeast corner of Bloor and St. George streets for graduate stu-dents. It was not, however, until Graduate House opened in 2000, with its over 420 places and with its large steel "O" dramatically hovering over the street at the corner of Spadina Avenue and Harbord Street, that the

Vincent Massey and Claude Bissell, president, with a model of Massey College, September 1963

university added significantly to its accommodations for graduate students.

The university library system also had to expand in order to provide facilities for the expected increase in the number of graduate students. A separate research library for the humanities and social sciences was a high priority for President Bissell. The university had not originally planned a major expansion north of Harbord Street, but it became clear that this was the only reasonable possibility for a major library complex. The New York firm of Warner, Burns, Toan & Lunde proposed a bold cluster of linked structures, focusing on an enormous triangle-shaped building, each side of which would be 330 feet long—the length of a Canadian football field. The John P. Robarts Research Library, the complex's central triangular area, was officially opened in 1973 and named after the Ontario premier who authorized the project. The monumental, sixteen-story building (including underground floors) is said to be the largest academic library building in the world. The south wing of the library complex houses the Faculty of Information and the north wing one of the most spectacular sights in the university—a rare book library with an awe-inspiring six-story open interior and soaring wood shelving. A third wing, imagined to the west in the original master plan, has been approved in principle by the university.

The colleges and departments also expanded their collections. New libraries were built at University College and at Victoria, Trinity, and St. Michael's colleges. At the end of World War Two, the Toronto library system had only five hundred thousand books and was ranked thirty-sixth among university libraries in North America. By 1965 it was ranked eleventh, and by the end of the century, it had eight million volumes and ranked second only to Harvard University in acquisitions.

The 1970s and 1980s were difficult years for the University of Toronto, as for other Canadian universities. The Ontario government wanted to control its expenditures on universities, which had grown between 1965 and 1969 from 1 percent to about 10 percent of its budget. Within the first six months of university president John Evans taking office in 1972, the government imposed a freeze on all new provincially funded capital expenditures, including the renovation of old buildings. A fundraising campaign in the latter half of the 1970s was used primarily for renovations, including a comprehensive restoration of University College. It also funded a new athletic center on Harbord Street and the Koffler Student Services Centre incorporating the former Toronto Reference Library on College Street, and helped with the initial funding of a new Earth Sciences Centre on the west campus. Financial constraint continued—even intensified—after Evans left office in 1978. The new president, James Ham, spent much of his five years in office cutting budgets.

Despite the financial difficulties the university established a new college, Woodsworth College, in 1974 for part-time students. Until then, part-time students had been under the umbrella of the extension division, which had operated successfully since President Falconer's day. The extension division, today called the School of Continuing Studies, with newly renovated quarters on the west side of St. George Street, near Bloor Street, continues its successful outreach program. At first operating out of several historic houses located across the road from the School of Continuing Studies, Woodsworth College continued to grow, and a new award-winning building designed by Kuwabara Payne McKenna Blumberg Architects in association with Barton Myers Associates and completed in 1992, imaginatively combines the historic houses with an old drill hall. An architecturally ambitious Woodsworth tower residence for some of its many full-time students—the college is no longer just for part-time students—recently opened at the southeast corner of Bloor and St. George streets.

The Earth Sciences Centre, located between Huron Street and Spadina Avenue and accommodating botany, forestry, geology, and related disciplines, was officially opened during President George Connell's tenure in 1989. A. J. Diamond's thoughtful design incorporated Bancroft Avenue as a pleasant pedestrian street.

President Connell, who took office in 1984, inherited a demoralized university. He was, however, able to lay the foundations for his successor Robert Prichard's successful ten-year presidency in the 1990s. Connell supported increased research at the hospitals, introduced long-range

President Robert Prichard (rear) and his four vice-presidents in the fall of 1999; from left to right: Michael Finlayson, Jon Dellandrea, Heather Munroe-Blum, and Adel Sedra

budgeting, and restructured the university's governing process to give the faculty a greater role and therefore a greater stake in the university. A turning point in the history of the university was the Nobel Prize in chemistry awarded to John Polanyi in 1986. In part because of Polanyi, both the federal and provincial governments started to fund "centres of excellence" instead of limiting their funding to a formula based on student enrollment. Funding based on quality gave the University of Toronto a natural advantage.

Recent Years

Robert Prichard became president in 1990 and made a great contribution to the physical shape of the university. He had taken an elective course in modern architecture while an undergraduate at Swarthmore College in Pennsylvania, which sparked a lifelong interest in building design and construction. He and his four talented vice-presidents were able to raise large sums in a fundraising campaign, which was primarily devoted to funding academic chairs. At the end of Prichard's tenure in 2000, the university had raised $700 million, and during his successor Robert Birgeneau's presidency, the campaign reached $1 billion. Impressive fundraising activity has continued under President David Naylor, who took office in 2005.

Over the past fifteen years, the university has been both acquiring existing buildings and actively constructing new ones on the St. George campus as well as at Scarborough and Mississauga. For some years the sight of numerous cranes has been a feature of life on all three campuses. One can see the extraordinary growth by observing recent changes at various vantage points on the downtown campus.

From the corner of University Avenue and College Street, for example, one can see a number of existing buildings purchased by the university, such as 500 University Avenue for rehabilitation science and the former Board of Education buildings on College Street for the faculties of nursing and medicine. On the north side of College Street is the Leslie L. Dan Pharmacy Building designed by Lord Norman Foster and opened in 2006 and the Terrence Donnelly Centre for Cellular and Biomolecular Research designed by Behnisch, Behnisch & Partner of Stuttgart, Germany, opened in 2005. Further west is the Bahen Centre for Information Technology of 2002, designed by Diamond + Schmitt Architects. The immense MaRS complex on the south side of College Street, stretching from University Avenue to Elizabeth Street—which incorporates the original 1913 Toronto General Hospital building—is presently being completed and brings entrepreneurs and scientists together in one setting.

Further north, at the corner of Bloor Street and Queen's Park one can see Daniel Libeskind's striking addition to the Royal Ontario Museum, once an integral part of the university and still closely associated with it; Victoria College's Isabel Bader Theatre designed by Lett/Smith Architects; and new additions to the Royal Conservatory of Music, by Kuwabara Payne McKenna Blumberg Architects. At the time of writing, the university has commissioned a master plan for the Faculty of Law, by Hariri Pontarini, that will embrace the historic Flavelle House.

Along St. George Street are new buildings constructed over the past twenty years, such as the Zeidler Partnership's Joseph L. Rotman School of Management, completed in 1995, and three new residences—for Innis, Woodsworth, and University colleges—as well as additions to the chemistry building and the previously mentioned Bahen Centre for Information Technology, both by Diamond + Schmitt. The university has also acquired the existing Medical Arts Building at the northwest corner of St. George and Bloor streets, which will accommodate humanities disciplines. From the corner of St. George and Harbord streets one can see Graduate House, designed by the Pritzker Prize–winning Thom Mayne of the U.S. firm Morphosis.

There have also been important changes in the physical landscape of the university. In 1994 Judy Matthews, a philanthropic alumna, donated funds to transform St. George Street with a new urban design infrastructure supporting pedestrian flow, and with flowerbeds and trees. It was the start of a comprehensive program to improve the quality of public, open space and enhance the physical beauty of the university. The university subsequently launched its Open Space Master Plan initiative, "Investing in the Landscape," which aims to knit together the campus, create more green space with more trees and less concrete, eliminate cars on the Front Campus, and recognize the importance of pedestrians. The new entrance gates at College Street and the redesign of King's College Road to the front campus were part of the first phase of this plan.

The planning and urban design process at the university has also changed dramatically over the past decade. The university and the city of Toronto concluded an agreement in 1997—with the support of local residents' groups who normally oppose development—to permit the use of twenty-eight specific sites on the downtown campus for future expansion. In determining the development sites, the university agreed that future buildings conform to certain urban design guidelines rather than density provisions. These criteria became the evaluative tool for development permissions in the City of Toronto Official Plan and remain in force today. At the same time, the university established a physical planning and design advisory committee, the Design Review Committee, to review design policy, participate in architect selection, and consider the design of future university buildings as well as revisions to the university's master plans.

Planning for future growth has been a priority in recent years. In 2000, the university prepared plans to expand enrollment on all three campuses to meet the future growth of demand for university places for children of the postwar baby boomers. The principal growth has been at Scarborough and Mississauga, where enrollment has increased by at least 50 percent on each campus.

The Scarborough and Mississauga campuses had been established in a rural setting with significant conservation lands in their midst, and so on these campuses expansion is limited to certain areas that will not impact the flood plains or the conservation lands. The increased enrollment and recent expansion on both campuses have led to institutions that are each now as large as many other North American liberal arts colleges or universities. As on the St. George campus, many of the new structures at Mississauga and Scarborough, such as the Communication, Culture and Technology Building at Mississauga and the Academic Resource Center at Scarborough, are by award-winning architects with strong national, even international reputations.

The University of Toronto started out in the early nineteenth century in a pastoral setting far outside the city limits, growing its own vegetables for the students in residence. It is now an intensely urban institution embedded in and integral to Toronto's dense downtown and to the economy of the city and the province. The Greater Toronto area today possesses one of the largest populations in North America, destined, according to some estimates, to become the fourth largest North American city outside of Mexico, after New York, Chicago, and Los Angeles. Almost half the immigration to Canada ends up in the Toronto area.

The University of Toronto flows into the city and the city flows through the campus. It is often difficult to tell where the university ends, with its many buildings south of College Street and north of Bloor Street. As an urban entity, the University of Toronto is in this respect like New York University rather than Columbia University. The growth of the many affiliated teaching hospitals throughout the city likewise contributes to this effect. The two suburban campuses, Scarborough and Mississauga, also started life in rural settings, but like the St. George campus are becoming part of the urban landscape.

While there is no prevailing architectural style at the university—in part because each denominational college was and still is responsible for the design of its buildings—it contains some of the finest architecture in Canada, starting with Frederic Cumberland's masterpiece, University College, and including ninety heritage sites on the three campuses. In the coming years, there will continue to be growth, particularly at the suburban campuses, and the panorama of designs and styles will also continue. Campus planning has become of increasing importance in recent years, and on the St. George campus, the Open Space Master Plan and the incremental landscape projects have the potential to be the "glue" that binds this architecturally diverse campus together.

I trust that readers will enjoy their tour of the campuses of the University of Toronto through Larry Richards's descriptions and through their own walks through the campuses. The university's diverse treasury of buildings provides the opportunity to learn much about the history of architecture in Canada and beyond. Moreover, readers will learn about more than just architecture, because the history of the University of Toronto mirrors the history of Toronto, the history of Ontario, and the history of Canada.

WALK ONE: THE HISTORIC CAMPUS

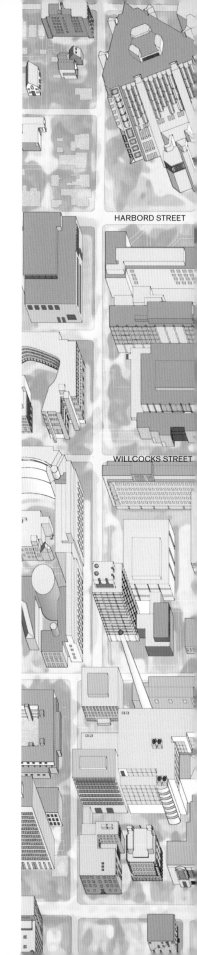

HARBORD STREET

WILLCOCKS STREET

HOSKIN AVENUE

BACK CAMPUS

QUEEN'S PARK

2b

2a

2d

2c

TOWER ROAD

6

4

5

HART HOUSE CIRCLE

3

2

8

ST. GEORGE STREET

QUEEN'S PARK CRESCENT WEST

12a

11

12

12b

13

KING'S COLLEGE CIRCLE

FRONT CAMPUS

1

7

9

15

14

16

10

17a

17b

17

17g

18

17e

17f

KING'S COLLEGE ROAD

17c

17d

1

COLLEGE STREET

Walk One: The Historic Campus

The city of Toronto is densely built and, in its collective mindset, overtly modernist. It has also become a city of towers, with scores of residential high-rise structures surrounding the University of Toronto's downtown St. George campus. In this context the university's central, historic campus with its substantial masonry buildings, courtyards, lawns, playing fields, and mature trees is not only distinctive but, increasingly, of great value as a network of public open spaces. Here we find an oasis of calm amidst metropolitan fervor.

The precinct also has a remarkable concentration of heritage structures: the city officially lists twenty-one of the buildings discussed in this walk as historically or architecturally significant, which leads to frequent discussion of the area as a virtual museum of architecture. Given the quality and range of designs—from the moody, mysterious University College (1859) to the Bauhaus-austere Mechanical Engineering Building (1948) to the comforting, embracing Morrison Pavilion (2003)—the sense of a museum starts moving from the virtual to the palpable.

In his introduction, Martin Friedland recounts the establishment of the university in 1850 and its gradual settling of the forest lands to the north of the town of York, now the city of Toronto. Completely urbanized today, the campus nevertheless retains gentle traces from a century and a half ago. One of my favorite escapes is to sit on the porch of Cumberland House at 33 St. George Street, the house that Frederic Cumberland, architect of University College, designed for his family at the end of the 1850s. Looking across the fenced-in lawn, I picture a game of croquet underway and horse-drawn carriages clicking along nearby College Avenue (now College Street). From the second floor of the house, Cumberland could have gazed through the trees northward and seen his magnificent new creation, University College.

Courtyard, Sir Daniel Wilson Residence

Alumni Gates and King's College Road

While the world of the 1850s seems far off, the buildings and landscapes that survive from that era and the 150 years since help us imagine the past, fantasize about it, and in turn better understand our complicated present. Encased by modern, vertical Toronto, the university's historic precinct is a didactic jewel that continues to instruct.

1. Alumni Gates, King's College Road, and King's College Circle

Andropogon Associates, Ltd., in association with Elias + Associates Landscape Architects, 2003

The University of Toronto's grand "front door" on College Street is marked by limestone-clad gateposts that are gradually being enveloped in wisteria. The lower parts of the gateposts are heavily rusticated, similar to the base of the neighboring Mining Building. Although constructed recently, the Alumni Gates, commemorating the one hundredth anniversary of the University of Toronto Alumni Association, and the entrance plaza have quickly taken on an aura of formality and tradition, reinforced by the stone paving of King's College Road as well as by the handsome walkways and seating, elegant lampposts, and additional tree planting that were completed at the same time as the new gates. Together, these elements strengthen the axial view north to King's College Circle and University College that has existed ever since the old Magnetic and Meteorological Observatory, which blocked the view, was dismantled in 1908.

University College originally had a picturesque, meandering approach from the southeast, across Taddle Creek. In the 1860s or 1870s, the university built a road from College Avenue (now College Street), on axis with University College, but it only extended about halfway as far north as today's King's College Road. Early photographs of the area show unpaved dirt and gravel roadways in front of University College, forming a squarish circle. For many years this area contained a cricket pitch. In landscape architect Bryant Fleming's 1917 "Preliminary Plan for the Landscape Improvement and General Expansion for the University of Toronto," this large open space is labeled "The Green," while contemporary maps refer to it simply as the "Front Campus."

Although Fleming asserted that the primary entrance to the campus should be from the east and fully integrated with Queen's Park, he somewhat begrudgingly accepted that "at present it [King's College Road entrance] is probably conceded to be the most important." For King's College Road, Fleming proposed "properly located walks paralleling the roadway" and suggested that double rows of trees "considerately spaced should be so planted as to form an avenue of vision to and from Main Building [University College]." He envisioned a new plaza at the north end of this avenue, next to Convocation Hall. Interestingly, he also focused on the south vista from University College, calling for a visual termination to that axis on the south side of College Street. He imagined "the approach from the north being axial with the tower of Main Building, and to the south upon some strong architectural monument or motif, located across College Street upon land condemned for such purposes."

Fleming's 1917 vision was rekindled a few years ago by Philadelphia-based Andropogon Associates, Ltd., the landscape architects for Alumni Gates and King's College Road. Their work was part of a much larger initiative for the area that included the redesign of King's College Circle as part of the university's ambitious Open Space Master Plan. Their concept proposed that the Front Campus lawn within King's College Circle would be retained as a playing field but also become more formal—a pure circle—and that automobile parking around it would be eliminated. Andropogon Associates, Ltd., also designed a new plaza at the north end of King's College Road, between Convocation Hall and the Medical Sciences Building, in the exact location that Fleming had foreseen; but, alas, the landscape architects did not engage the notion of a southern plaza across College Street. For now, the distant silhouette of Toronto's CN Tower must suffice as a termination of the south axis from University College.

If the more formalized King's College Circle and Convocation Hall plaza are developed, the heart of the campus will gain the full pedestrian emphasis and further visual refinement that it deserves.

University College and the Front Campus

2. University College *Cumberland & Storm, 1859*
Restoration and renovation *David B. Dick, 1892*
Restoration and renovation *Wilson Newton, Roberts Duncan, and Eric Arthur, 1979*
Laidlaw Wing *Mathers & Haldenby, 1964*

Towered, turreted, majestic University College is arguably the most important structure on the St. George campus, both historically and architecturally. The university approved funding for the building in February 1856; Frederic Cumberland, a member of the University of Toronto senate, and the highly artistic William Storm were appointed as the project architects the same month; construction started on October 4, 1856; and the building, designed in the rugged Romanesque-revival style, rooted in medieval architecture of the eleventh and twelfth centuries, opened three years later on October 4, 1859.

Although major changes to the natural landscape have occurred over the years, causing "U.C.," as it is affectionately known, to forfeit the full power of its original picturesque reading, the building continues to have great significance as the university's iconic set piece. In 1968 University College was designated by the National Historic Sites and Monuments Board, sealing its status as a national treasure.

In his authoritative book *A Not Unsightly Building: University College and Its History,* Douglas Richardson reminds us that, in the early 1850s, Toronto was hardly a city but rather "a small town still" of about thirty thousand people with

Dragon, east stair, University College

"only fields and scattered houses north of Dundas" and the university grounds "set apart in the semi-rural outskirts of the city." (The city was also still rebuilding following the devastating fire that destroyed four entire blocks of its core in 1849.) The completion of University College brought substantial construction activity and, finally, fame and architectural glory to sleepy, Victorian Toronto. The building became a key stop for prominent visitors, including Edward, Prince of Wales, who included it in his 1860 itinerary. By 1883 horse-drawn street cars rattled along College Avenue just south of University College, and Toronto was in the midst of major urban expansion to the north and west. University College and its pastoral setting had become an island in the midst of a bustling city with a population of more than eighty thousand (see birds-eye view, page 10).

Cumberland & Storm's "First Study" for University College shows a layout inspired by Oxford and Cambridge universities, forming a large rectangular quadrangle. As the design developed, considerable influence seeped in from John Ruskin and the Dublin architects Deane & Woodward—in particular from their 1855 to 1859 work on the University Museum, Oxford, with which Cumberland & Storm were quite familiar. It seems that the University of Toronto and the architects wanted to avoid the Gothic style, which was strongly associated with churches and denominational colleges; they thought the rugged Romanesque approach was more suitable for Toronto's northern climate than the more intricate Gothic.

The resulting building was U-shaped with a quadrangle opening to the north to what would become known as the "Back Campus." In addition to its massive main tower and arched entrance on the south, University College was distinguished by the circular chemistry lab at the southwest corner, now the lovely Croft Chapter House. Cumberland & Storm designated stone as the building material, and about a third of it is made of stone, incorporating substantial amounts of sandstone from Georgetown, west of Toronto, along with stone imported from Ohio and France. Due to budget restraints the remainder was constructed mostly of brick, although the building displays an astonishing array of sculptural, carved ornament in stone and wood along with spectacular polychromed tile floors and beautiful stained glass. Indeed, one must explore the interior to fully appreciate this masterful work of architecture.

TOP: *Cloister at University College*
BOTTOM: *University College Quadrangle*

On February 14, 1890, a fire broke out in the southeast corner of University College and spread rapidly, following an accident involving kerosene lamps. The following Sunday, more than fifty thousand Torontonians showed up to survey the disaster. Although many interior spaces were destroyed in the eastern portions, the stone structure survived, and the university, provincial government, and broader community immediately rallied to restore the magnificent building. David B. Dick, a talented architect who was born in Scotland and trained in Edinburgh before moving to Toronto in 1873 (where he became university architect and designed the new university library), was placed in charge of the restoration in September, 1890, and University College was fully reoccupied by January 1892. With minor exceptions, the overall configuration of the restored structure changed very little. U.C.'s burned-out Convocation Hall was replaced with needed lecture rooms and offices, and a new boiler house and men's lavatory wing was added in the quadrangle at the north end of the east wing. Dick also deviated somewhat from the original high Victorian style of Cumberland & Storm, particularly for the east wing, adding a then more fashionable late-Victorian layer.

In 1964 the yellow brick and buff stone, neo-Norman-style Laidlaw Wing, housing the College Library, was built across the north end of the U-shaped building. It was designed by Mathers & Haldenby, a Toronto firm that was passed down through two generations in both families and exemplified "Ontario establishment" in the fullest sense with its low-key, conservative architecture. The new wing finally enclosed the quadrangle in a manner similar in plan to Cumberland & Storm's "First Study," but it is uncomfortably elephantine in scale and lacks sophistication and finesse in terms of proportion and detailing. Along the Laidlaw Wing's south-facing arcade is the University of Toronto Art Centre, housing the university's extensive art collection.

2a. University College Union

1885 *(architect unknown)*
Addition *Darling & Pearson, 1923*
Renovations *Stinson Montgomery & Sisam Architects, 1987*

Originally a fine late-Victorian residence, this building was first occupied by George H. Watson QC, partner in the successful law firm of Watson, Smoke & Masten, Barristors & Solicitors, and later by Lt. Col. Frederic Nicholls, president of the Canadian General Electric Company. The facade facing St. George Street displays what is sometimes referred to as "Toronto bay and gable" style and presents a projecting third-floor gable clad in fluted shingles. An intricate wrought-iron fence is found in front of the house.

In 1916 the university acquired the building for the University College Women's Union, and in 1922 to 1923, architects Darling & Pearson completed a major addition to the east. The union, which now serves both male and female students, supports a broad range of University College activities and includes the Helen Gardiner Playhouse. With the recent construction of Morrison Hall to the south, a pleasant landscaped pathway has resulted between the buildings that reinforces the university's commitment to enhancing the pedestrian experience.

Whitney Hall

2b. Whitney Hall
Mathers & Haldenby (with John M. Lyle as consulting architect), 1931
Ferguson Wing *Mathers & Haldenby, 1960*

Whitney Hall is named for the wealthy lumber baron Edward C. Whitney, brother of Sir James P. Whitney, who was premier of Ontario from 1905 to 1914. The residence was originally for women only but is now coeducational and accommodates 250 students in four houses composed around a well-defined quadrangle that opens on the east to the Back Campus.

In 1930 St. George Street formed the western boundary of the campus. To establish a consistent style and character to the public face of the institution, the administration had mandated since 1920 that all new buildings along College and St. George streets be "Georgian in character," and Mathers & Haldenby—in consultation with John M. Lyle, one of Canada's outstanding architects of the first half of the twentieth century—responded accordingly with this red brick structure that has finely articulated doorways, railings, and lanterns.

In 1960 a wing designed by Mathers & Haldenby was added at the southeast corner, seamlessly continuing the same Georgian-revival vocabulary used thirty years earlier.

2c. Sir Daniel Wilson Residence *Mathers & Haldenby, 1954*

Sir Daniel Wilson Residence

Now coeducational, the Sir Daniel Wilson Residence was first opened by University College fifty-five years ago, for men. It is announced on St. George Street with a large clock tower that rises above a portico marking the main entrance. The building honors Sir Daniel Wilson, president of University College from 1880 to 1892 and later first president of the newly federated University of Toronto.

The Sir Daniel Wilson Residence was completed twenty-five years after neighboring Whitney Hall. Mathers & Haldenby again employed the conservative Georgian-revival style, but the two buildings are quite different: Whitney Hall is red brick while Sir Daniel Wilson is built of yellow buff brick; and whereas Whitney Hall forms a pleasing, square quadrangle, Sir Daniel Wilson's quadrangle is ill-defined and drifts ambiguously toward the main University College building. In 2005, when Morrison Hall was added directly to the north, Sir Daniel Wilson's Ferguson Dining Hall (the north wing of the quasi-quadrangle) was renovated and expanded to serve both residences.

2d. Morrison Hall *Zeidler Partnership Architects, 2005*

The realization of coeducational Morrison Hall in 2005 ended a long, tortured discussion about where and how University College might add another student residence. Each site the college considered generated a heated debate about preserving green space and existing views, retaining mature trees, and the always contentious matter of architectural style. Eventually, a very tight infill site fronting on St. George Street was selected for the 270-bed residence, to the north of and adjacent to Sir Daniel Wilson.

Morrison Hall's thirteen-story, zinc-clad tower, rising from a two-story yellow brick podium that integrates seamlessly with Sir Daniel Wilson, evokes the gray blue of neighboring slate roofs. The tower steps back three times near the top to refer to nearby collegiate Gothic structures such as the Soldiers' Tower, its

Morrison Hall

volumetric twin to the east. A large, decorative gate thoughtfully screens the delivery area from St. George Street. The residence provides comfortable quarters for undergraduate students, and many aspects of Zeidler Partnership Architects' design are thoughtful; but, finally, what resulted from many years of wrangling about site, context, and style is uninspired, even lacking final flourishes at the top that could have related to the iron finials pointing skyward from its magical mothership, the original University College next door.

3. Louis B. Stewart Observatory (Students' Union)

Cumberland & Storm, 1855; moved and rebuilt, 1908

The Louis B. Stewart Observatory, now housing the offices of the Students' Union, was originally located south of King's College Circle as part of the Toronto Magnetic and Meteorological Observatory, completed in 1855 in a mildly Venetian style by the same architects selected one year later for University College. A landscaped area commemorating the original facility, which consisted of a main structure with a domed corner tower and smaller surrounding buildings within a walled compound, is located at the northeast corner of the Sanford Fleming Building.

In 1908 the observatory was dismantled to make way for the northward extension of King's College Road. The materials were reused to build the Louis B.

Louis B. Stewart Observatory (Students' Union)

Stewart Observatory in its present location, including a tower similar to the original one. The structure served meteorological and astronomical studies until 1953. It now houses the Students' Union offices and has become a rallying point for student concerns, frequently sporting creative graffiti. On the building's east face a wall-mounted relief designed by Johnny Koo and Bruce Parsons and incorporating a smashed bicycle commemorates "Those Who Gave Their Lives for Democracy on June 4, 1989 in Tiananmen Square, Beijing."

4. Hart House *Sproatt & Rolph, 1919*

Hart House impresses through the beauty of its materials, detailing, and craftsmanship. The construction of this fine student facility at the beginning of the twentieth century was made possible by its generous patron, Vincent Massey, the first Canadian-born governor general of Canada. The Massey family had acquired considerable wealth via the Massey Manufacturing Company, later merged as Massey-Harris. Hart Almerrin Massey, who had serious interests in efficiency through design, died in 1896, and the philanthropic funding that he left enabled the creation of the Massey Foundation. However, it was Vincent Massey, Hart's grandson, who was particularly interested in the cultural role of progressive architecture. A graduate of Toronto's University College and Balliol College, Oxford, Vincent Massey became convinced that the University of Toronto needed a central student facility and in 1910 confirmed Massey Estate funding, along with YMCA support, for an ambitious new kind of campus center.

From 1910 to 1919, Massey closely monitored and participated in design and construction decisions for Hart House, named in honor of his grandfather. He was also influential in shaping matters of use, social interaction, and governance at the new campus center. (For him "common fellowship" meant "men." Women were not admitted to Hart House on equal terms until 1972.) A lengthy dedicatory inscription at the east end of the first floor corridor records the aspirations of the facility. A passage from it reads:

> The prayer of the founders is that Hart House…may serve in the generations to come the highest interests of this university by drawing into a common fellowship the members of the several colleges and faculties, and by gathering into a true society the teacher and the student, the graduate and the undergraduate; further that the members of Hart House may discover within its walls the true education that is to be found in good fellowship, in friendly disputation and debate, in the conversation of wise and earnest men, in music, pictures and the play, in the casual book, in sports and games and the mastery of the body.

As architectural historians William Dendy and William Kilbourn have claimed, Hart House is perhaps Canada's finest example of beaux arts Gothic-revival. The building's planning is superb with common rooms in the south and west wings, athletic functions in the north wing, the Great Hall to the east, and a theater placed underground below the narrow, central quadrangle. Hart House embodies the picturesque qualities of Oxford and Cambridge, balancing small-scale comfort with moments of real grandeur.

The Great Hall, designed for serving meals for up to three hundred people, is covered by a hammerbeam roof of steel and oak. A monumental, traceried south window features armorial glass honoring ten of the university's benefactors and college founders. Below the window are panels bearing the arms of the British Royal Family, along with arms of fifty-one universities in the British Empire of the early twentieth century. Rising from the south-end dais is a mysterious "corkscrew" Gothic stair tower that originally led to the second-floor Faculty Union Senior Common Room (now the receiving room and bar of the Gallery Grill, a favored gourmet dining destination on campus). Running along the top of the oak paneling is an inscription chosen by Massey from John Milton's *Areopagitica*—an attack on censorship of the press.

Visitors should not miss the civilized Lecture Room, the Library, Map Room, Reading Room, East Common Room, and the Music Room, the latter featuring an exquisite ceiling structure of British Columbia cedar. The tiny Chapel, on the first floor, features windows containing fragments of stained glass from ruined churches in France, Belgium, and Italy. The architectural feast continues with an intimate, five-hundred-seat theater tucked into the basement level, under the central courtyard. Interestingly, it was the location for a lecture by the famous American architect, Frank Lloyd Wright, on November 30, 1949.

Hart House, University College, and the 1924 Soldiers' Tower and arched colonnade that link the two, contribute two sides of Hart House Circle, a space loosely defined on the south by the Gerstein Science Information Centre. The Queen's Park Crescent West overpass, constructed in 1949, forms the rather rude eastern boundary of this historic zone, which was originally contiguous with Queen's Park. Ideally, the high-speed overpass should be taken down, allowing Hart House Circle and Queen's Park to once again flow gently together.

Today Hart House embraces superb theatrical performances, literary activities, and an outstanding collection of Canadian art. It remains a vibrant, collegial place and continues to fulfill the vision of its forward-thinking patron. Indeed, the claim in the University Board of Governors' 1921 book on Hart House that "the passage of time will leave the building more and more beautiful" resonates as fact.

Hart House, Great Hall

Soldiers' Tower and Hart House

5. Soldiers' Tower *Sproatt & Rolph, 1924*
Modifications *Mathers & Haldenby, 1949*

Located at the northwest corner of Hart House Circle, the Gothic-style Soldiers'
Tower and its carillon were sponsored by the university's Alumni Federation,
now known as the University of Toronto Alumni Association, to honor students
and alumni who lost their lives in World War One. The cornerstone was laid on
November 11, 1919, the same day that Hart House was officially opened.

The composition of Soldiers' Tower is more complex than it first appears.
Standing at the south end of Tower Road, it links University College and Hart
House. To the east it is tied to the latter by a volume containing the stair that leads

to the Muniment Room, a vaulted space halfway up the tower that contains archival material and memorabilia related to both world wars. Joined to the tower's base is a colonnade with large stone tablets bearing the inscribed names of members of the university who perished in World War One. The base of the tower incorporates a fan-vaulted passageway, whose side walls were redesigned in 1949 by Mathers & Haldenby and inscribed with the names of members of the university killed in World War Two. The sophistication of the Soldiers' Tower was duly recognized in 1990, when it was awarded a City of Toronto Urban Design Award.

The tower's carillon was not dedicated until 1927. The first carillon had twenty-three bells, with nineteen added in 1952. The tower was renovated, and major improvements were made to the carillon in the mid-1970s, increasing the total number of bells to fifty-one.

6. Wycliffe College *David B. Dick, 1891*
Convocation Hall *George M. Miller, 1902*
Refectory, library, and residence hall addition *Gordon & Helliwell, 1907*
Principal's residence and new chapel *Gordon & Helliwell, 1911*
New library (Leonard Hall) *Chapman & Oxley, 1930*

Wycliffe College

Named for the Oxford theologian, priest, and professor John Wycliffe, Wycliffe College is an Evangelical Anglican graduate school of theology that prepares students for the ministry. The seminary was founded in 1877 as the Protestant Episcopal Divinity School by the Church Association of the Diocese of Toronto, a lay evangelical group at St. James Cathedral that championed the doctrinal points of the English Reformation.

The school moved to the University of Toronto area in 1881 and affiliated with the university in 1885. Becoming a federated college in 1889, it constructed its first building on campus in 1891, a red brick Victorian ensemble that speaks of austerity and sobriety. A closer look reveals small architectural delights, however, such as the highly detailed brickwork surrounding the large windows to the left of the main entrance fronting on Hoskin Avenue.

The elegant 1930 library addition at the southwest corner, Leonard Hall, seems curious at first, because its collegiate Gothic style and Credit Valley stone cladding are more akin to nearby Hart House than to Wycliffe College itself. The intention was to eventually replace Wycliffe's older, modest brick buildings with new stone buildings in the collegiate Gothic style, but this vision was never realized.

Besides Leonard Hall, Wycliffe College has numerous interior spaces worth visiting, including the Soward Reading Room, Founder's Chapel, Sheraton Hall, and the Refectory, this latter space capturing the sense of simplicity and common moral life that are deeply valued by the Wycliffe community.

7. Gerstein Science Information Centre

Original library (Sigmund Samuel Building) *David B. Dick, 1892*
Bookstack wing *Darling & Pearson, 1909*
North wing *Mathers & Haldenby, 1954*
Morrison Pavilion *Diamond + Schmitt Architects, 2003*

Gerstein Science Information Centre, Morrison Pavilion

This sprawling complex houses Canada's largest academic science and medicine library. The development of the center spans 111 years, from the highly eclectic 1892 structure, facing on King's College Circle, to the suave Morrison Pavilion of 2003, nestled into the ravine and facing the provincial legislative buildings.

The pivotal piece of the composition is the original "New University Library" designed by David B. Dick, now the Sigmund Samuel Building. By the 1880s the university urgently needed a new library, having outgrown the one housed in University College; the devastating fire that destroyed University College in 1890 made this even more imperative. Dick's cruciform plan for the new structure included a tower (influenced by Kelso Abbey in Scotland, Dick's place of birth) that marked an exuberantly sculpted entrance porch. These elements can still be enjoyed today, although the original gorgeous entrance has been demoted to an emergency exit. The magnificent five-story bookstack wing by Darling & Pearson was completed in 1909. Its structural glass floors allow natural light to flow down through the building. A major wing by Mathers & Haldenby, clad

1909 Bookstack wing, Gerstein Science Information Centre

in Queenston limestone, was added at the north in 1954. Together with the earlier buildings, it functioned as the University Library until 1973, when Robarts Library was completed.

The recent Morrison Pavilion, providing 650 additional study spaces, was imaginatively grafted onto the east side of the center's north wing. An octagonal tower, topped by four abstract copper-clad planes, authoritatively completes the 1954 entry axis and serves as a strong orientation point. A copper-clad vault runs the length of the slender pavilion, whose walls are faced in rough-cut stone, giving the library an appropriately weighty aspect. Contrasting with this, alternating thin planes of gray glass seem to defy gravity and float across the stone face. The elongated pavilion feels entirely sympathetic with the early parts of the complex without being historicist.

8. Volunteers' Monument

McDougall & Skae (site planning); Mavor & Co. (Robert Reid, sculptor), 1870
Restoration *Spencer R. Higgins, 2008*

This major monument—Toronto's first public sculpture—commemorates Canadians lost in the June 1866 skirmish with the Fenians at the Battle of Ridgeway. The story leading to the monument starts during the American Civil War, when, during

Volunteers' Monument

a crisis in British-American relations, the threat of an American attack on Canada emerged. This led to the formation of volunteer rifle companies, including one at University College in 1862. In 1866, after the Civil War, a new threat appeared from the Fenians—Irish-Americans who sought to revenge accumulated wrongs to their native Ireland and selected nearby English Canada as a target. The Fenians, some eight hundred strong, crossed the Niagara River in force, and a Toronto "Queen's Own Rifles K Company," which included the University College group of volunteer faculty members and students, joined troop trains going to the border. A battle unfolded at Ridgeway, and although the Fenians finally withdrew and retreated across the border, three University College men were killed in the confusion.

The monument was financed through public subscription of one dollar per contributor and erected in 1870 in a sylvan setting that overlooked the now-buried Taddle Creek. What was built was much less ambitious than the vision put forward in 1869 by William Storm, who had proposed a brick caretaker's lodge, trees, and elaborate walkways leading to and surrounding the monument. Montreal sculptor Robert Reid eventually executed the Volunteers' Monument in the Italian Renaissance style, composed of a tiered, rectangular gray-brown sandstone pedestal with diagonal buttresses, on which white marble figures are displayed. The east figure symbolizes "Grief," the west, "Faith," and the north and south figures represent Canadian Volunteer riflemen. A statue of Britannia rises at the top.

9. Canadiana Building *Mathers & Haldenby, 1951*

Donated by Dr. Sigmund Samuel, a noted philanthropist, this building was originally known as the Archives and Canadiana Building and housed Samuel's extensive collection of Canadian decorative arts. (This superb collection is now displayed at the Sigmund Samuel Gallery of Canada at the Royal Ontario Museum, three blocks to

LEFT: *Canadiana Building, Sir John Graves Simcoe*
RIGHT: *McMurrich Building*

the north.) In 2008 the university's Centre for Criminology and the School of Public Policy and Governance moved into the building.

The Canadiana Building is curious architecturally. Presenting a stone-clad single volume capped by a sloping slate roof, it embodies Canadian architect John M. Lyle's plea from the 1920s onward for "solidity and simplicity" and a certain Canadian leitmotif. The four sculptures commanding the building's facade—figures of Samuel de Champlain, General James Wolfe, Sir John Graves Simcoe, and Sir Isaac Brock—were designed by Jacobine Jones and carved by Louic Temporale. They underscore Lyle's nationalizing agenda. Throughout, the detailing and materials represent an engaging mixture of classical and modern impulses, from the handsome front doors with circular motifs, to the precisely detailed staircase, to the zigzag-pattern, inlaid cork floor in the main room to the right.

This small but monumental building finally commands our attention, because it is so fascinatingly transitional in terms of style. It marks a mid-twentieth-century period in Canada when modernism was, for the most part, in the crevices and still far from full-blown.

10. McMurrich Building *Darling & Pearson, 1922*

Opened in 1923 as the Anatomy Building, the McMurrich Building today hosts various university divisions such as the Office of Campus and Facilities Planning, Office of Space Management, Office of Research Ethics, and Research Accounting. Its original setting was surely spectacular, along the ravine of Taddle

Creek, traces of which are still evident, particularly where the landscape rolls downward at the building's north end. The west face has been highly compromised by an unsympathetic stair tower and the abutting plaza of the Medical Sciences Building; aggressive renovations in 1977 sadly erased the original interiors.

Approaching the building from Queen's Park, one can appreciate what remains of this splendid structure. The grand east facade features massive anchoring end towers, with five soaring stone pilasters in between, an elegant rhythm of fenestration, and a subtle row of arches and stonework marching across the top edge of the building. The beautifully carved stone doorway has a pair of sumptuous oak doors.

11. J. Robert S. Prichard Alumni House
Mathers & Haldenby, 1958

J. Robert S. Prichard Alumni House

This foursquare stone building served as the home of the University of Toronto Press from 1958 to 1989, when the press moved to a commercial office building on Yonge Street. The university bookstore was also located here until 1985, when it moved to the Koffler Student Services Centre on College Street. In 2000 the building was named the J. Robert S. Prichard Alumni House to honor the university's thirteenth president and currently houses advancement and alumni-related divisions.

Executed in a mildly Canadian chateau style featuring a steep slate roof and numerous dormer windows, it is similar to the university's Canadiana Building, completed seven years earlier by the same architects.

12. School of Graduate Studies

Although master's degrees were first awarded in 1843 at King's College and the doctorate degree was offered starting in 1897, the School of Graduate Studies was not formally established until 1922, with three hundred students. Today there are more than thirteen thousand graduate students registered in approximately one hundred graduate degree programs, making it the largest graduate school in Canada. The School of Graduate Studies has administrative offices in two historic houses at 63 and 65 St. George Street.

LEFT: *65 St. George Street*
RIGHT: *Macdonald–Mowat House*

12a. 65 St. George Street *David B. Dick, 1891*

It is not entirely surprising to discover that the talented David B. Dick, designer of the university's first library, was the architect of this superb house at 65 St. George Street, a rambling brick and stone Tudor-inspired building that stretches deep into the block. It was built for John Bryce Kay, Jr., one of the founders of the John Kay and Son household furniture stores, and purchased by the university in 1954.

12b. Macdonald-Mowat House (63 St. George Street)
Nathaniel Dickey, builder, 1872

To really appreciate this house, one must stand at the south-facing front door and imagine the pastoral setting that spread before it in 1872. The fancy suburban villa combining Italianate and Second Empire styles must have impressed Sir John A. Macdonald, Canada's first prime minister (1867–73), who purchased the house from Nathaniel Dickey in 1876 and lived there for two years before serving again as prime minister (1878–91). It is interesting to think of Macdonald as a suburban neighbor of architect Frederic Cumberland, whose villa had been realized a few years before, just 820 feet (250 meters) to the south. In 1888 the Hon. Oliver Mowat, premier of Ontario from 1872 to 1896, bought the house and kept it until 1902. The Presbyterian Church in Canada has owned the house since 1910.

Knox College

13. Knox College *Chapman & McGiffin, 1915*

Presbyterian Knox College's first home was on Spadina Crescent and opened in 1875 (see One Spadina Crescent, page 154). The college moved to its present location, fronting on both St. George Street and King's College Circle, in 1915, where it plays a quiet but crucial role in defining the western edge of the vast Front Campus. The best views of Knox College are from the east, looking across King's College Circle at the grand chapel and library volumes.

The building's U-shaped configuration creates a memorable exterior space that is divided in half by a covered walkway, making two cloisters. Wrapping around these pleasing cloisters are student dormitory rooms, classrooms and offices, a magnificent library, and a glorious chapel. Frequently leased by the film industry as a set, Knox College's collegiate Gothic style is perhaps somewhat ponderous on the outside, but inside, the college's full architectural glory abounds.

The main entrance hall, off King's College Circle, is supported by a forest of elegant columns rising to exquisitely crafted fan vaults. Stone balustrades with tracery ring the mezzanine level. From the entrance hall one can go up to the chapel on the south or the Caven Library on the north, both featuring enormous windows of amber stained glass.

The handsomely landscaped Nona Macdonald Walkway runs along the south side of Knox College, leading to the university's Nona Macdonald Visitors Centre, which is tucked into the ground level of the college.

Knox College

Convocation Hall

14. Convocation Hall *Darling & Pearson, 1906*
Renovation and restoration *ERA Architects Inc., 2007–10*

The view of the connected Convocation and Simcoe halls from the northeast, diagonally across the sweeping Front Campus lawn, is a familiar and inspiring one. Together, these buildings gracefully anchor and enable the spatial flow around the southwest corner of King's College Circle. However, it was not always so: when completed in 1906, Convocation Hall stood alone without Simcoe Hall, and what became King's College Circle was then a horseshoe-shaped gravel road leading to University College. The approach to Convocation Hall was originally from the east (centered on the building's eastern apse) along Taddle Creek Road (where the Medical Sciences Building is now), and Convocation Hall was set back considerably from the evolving King's College Road as part of a V-shaped view corridor from College Street to University College.

The University of Toronto Alumni Association first promoted the idea of a large hall in memory of those fallen in the Fenian raids and the Boer War; the proposition subsequently expanded, and, by the time the cornerstone was laid in the summer of 1904, the university required government support beyond the generous funding provided by alumni. At the time, the hall's two thousand seats probably seemed extravagant. Today, however, with several thousand graduates passing through Convocation Hall annually with family and friends, multiple packed-to-the-rafters convocation ceremonies are held each year.

The designers of Convocation Hall, Darling & Pearson, had become Toronto's preeminent architecture firm, with Frank Darling recognized as the guiding light. He studied and trained in England during 1870 to 1873 before moving to Toronto. His name or his firm's name appears in conjunction with more projects at the University of Toronto than any other architect. Darling received the Royal Institute of British Architects' Gold Medal in 1915 and died in April 1923. His successor firm completed numerous buildings at the university, the Banting Institute of 1930 being the last. Frank Darling was fluent in many architectural styles. For Convocation Hall he chose the beaux arts style and followed through with rigorous execution. To some extent the building is modeled on the Sorbonne theater in Paris. The cylindrical, central auditorium space features a splendid dome. Considering its size, the hall has a remarkably intimate feel.

In 2007 the university launched an ambitious restoration and refurbishing project that will both bring back much of Convocation Hall's original dignity and propel it into the twenty-first century. Once again alumni are rallying to support this great building—typically one of the first and last grand architectural experiences of a student's University of Toronto years.

15. Simcoe Hall   *Darling & Pearson, 1924*

Simcoe Hall

Simcoe Hall, a long bar-shaped building running north-south behind and adjacent to Convocation Hall, houses the university's provost, president, and senior administration. Its primary facade, facing the southwest corner of King's College Circle, was astutely set at an angle to negotiate between the "bar" and the infill wing joining Convocation Hall. Darling & Pearson placed an elegantly scaled, templelike front at the bend, complete with a pediment and two pairs of engaged pilasters topped by Ionic capitals. A Palladian window graces the center of this lovely composition. From the entrance hall to the Council Chamber, interior spaces are dignified, well proportioned, and elegantly detailed.

16. Physical Geography Building

Darling & Pearson, 1925

Physical Geography Building

Originally called the Forestry Building, this stately three-story brick structure first stood next door to Cumberland House, two hundred feet (sixty-one meters) south of where it is now. In order to make room for the Galbraith Building in 1960, Forestry was moved northward on steel rollers and placed on foundation walls that were about three feet higher than the original ones and faced in brick instead of limestone, resulting in an unfortunate change in the proportional sense and appearance of the building, which now serves the Department of Geography. Stylistically a hybrid of Georgian and classical revival influences, the Physical Geography Building offers several architectural pleasures, from the pediment-adorned entrance to the stone quoining at the corners to the balustraded parapet.

17. Faculty of Applied Science and Engineering

Established in 1873 as the School of Practical Science, the Faculty of Applied Science and Engineering (FASE) now boasts 4,400 students, 219 faculty members, and 40,000 living alumni. FASE occupies 13 buildings on the St. George campus (most of which are discussed in this walk) and several off campus, including the large Institute for Aerospace Studies at the north edge of the city. The Bahen Centre for Information Technology is presented in Walk Four and the Centre for Cellular and Biomolecular Research (of which FASE is a joint venture partner) in Walk Six.

17a. Galbraith Building *Page & Steele Architects, 1960*

The Galbraith Building, named for John Galbraith, professor of engineering, principal of the Ontario School of Practical Science, and first dean of FASE, is the faculty's main administrative center.

Galbraith Building

Designed in the spare International Style, the building was composed as a kind of "square donut" around a courtyard. Its architecture is for the most part unremarkable, although the rational marking of the structural bays, particularly on the north side, where a rigorous rhythm of limestone-clad columns and dark-brown and light-brown brick infill occurs, is interesting. The courtyard itself, which was originally open to the main lobby but later modified at the west, still has a late-1950s feel, including a lively little cantilever stair at the north side.

A bold 1972 minimalist steel sculpture called *Becca's H* by Robert Murray stands in front of the Galbraith Building, and a terra-cotta frieze from the former red brick Engineering Building (which stood where the Medical Sciences Building is now) is displayed near the front entrance.

17b. Sanford Fleming Building   *Darling & Pearson, 1907*

From 1905 to 1908, the King's College Road area was a beehive of building activity. Convocation Hall was completed in 1906; the old observatory was dismantled in 1908, allowing the northern extension of King's College Road; and a new physics building, known now as the Sanford Fleming Building, was finished in 1907. Sir Sanford Fleming was chief engineer of the Intercolonial Railway of Canada from 1864 to 1876 and, in 1871, was appointed chief engineer on Canadian Pacific Railways surveys. He was instrumental in establishing the standardized, twenty-four-hour system of international time zones.

Sanford Fleming Building

Confidently executed in the beaux arts style, the Sanford Fleming Building originally had a U-shaped composition; following a fire that gutted the building in 1977, the inside of the U was filled in to make a student commons area. The most distinguished aspect of the building is the monumental east facade with its convex, semicircular volume rendered in yellow brick and limestone. This volume, which now houses the Engineering and Computer Science Library, originally contained a large lecture hall. Three pairs of grand doors that led to the hall were retained. At the *piano nobile* level, six pairs of Ionic columns rise to support a classical cornice.

17c. Wallberg Memorial Building
Page & Steele Architects, 1949

Wallberg Memorial Building

The Wallberg Memorial Building, which primarily serves the chemical engineering department, resulted from a bequest by Ida Marie Wallberg in 1933 to commemorate her brother, Emil Andrew Wallberg, who had been president of Canada Wire and Cable and died in 1929. The start of construction was delayed until after World War Two, and the building's design reflects a conflict

Mining Building

between essentially classical and modern directions. Along College Street we find symmetry in the facade, including a pair of identical entrances. Romanlike urn balustrades sit alongside modern, steel casement windows. Inside, mildly streamlined, wood-paneled lobbies hint that the architects were trying to look toward the 1950s.

17d. Mining Building
Francis Riley Heakes with Frank Darling, 1905

Just two years after designing the minor Mill Building (now called the Haultain Building) for the university, Francis Riley Heakes, chief architect of the Ontario Public Works Department and designer of the province's nearby Whitney Block, and Frank Darling were awarded the large, important commission for the Mining Building (originally called Chemistry and Mining Building) on College Street.

At the beginning of the twentieth century, this section of College Street was still on the outskirts of Toronto, but the street was becoming an important east-west artery, and the city was expected to rapidly expand westward. The location and grandeur of the Mining Building signaled and encouraged this westward expansion. Executed in a turn-of-the-century beaux arts style with a bilaterally symmetrical front facade and monumental brick columns, it followed architectural ambitions at Cornell University, the University of Pennsylvania, and Columbia University, where imposing schools of metallurgy and mineralogy had been constructed. Heakes and Darling's original plans included two wings at the east and west, which extended

LEFT: *Haultain Buidling*
RIGHT: *Haultain Building, window detail*

north to form a quadrangle. Due to budget constraints, however, the wings were not realized.

The Mining Building is now home to the Mineral Engineering Program, the Lassonde Institute for Engineering Geoscience, the Institute of Biomaterials and Biomedical Engineering, and the Canadian Mining Hall of Fame. The latter recognizes and honors legendary mine finders and builders that contributed to the vast Canadian mining industry.

17e. Haultain Building
Francis Riley Heakes with Frank Darling, 1903
Expansion and rebuilding *Craig & Madill, 1931*

One of the university's hidden treasures is the seventy-foot-square (twenty-one-meter-square) Edwardian style Haultain Building, which was originally called the Mill Building. Constructed of red brick, it was a milling building for the School of Practical Science, housing machinery for experiments on the mechanical processing of ores. In the early 1930s, several floors were added. In its present state, it feels like a piece of late-nineteenth-century Liverpool transported to Toronto, waiting for film crews to discover it.

Rosebrugh Building and Centre for Cellular and Biomolecular Research (right)

17f. Rosebrugh Building   *Darling & Pearson, 1920*

Originally known as the Electrical Building, the Rosebrugh Building is attached
to and architecturally similar to the 1909 Thermodynamics Building. An early
photograph (see page 25) shows the splendor of the Rosebrugh when it stood
proudly on Taddle Creek Road, which was removed in 2003 to make way for the
new Terrence Donnelly Centre for Cellular and Biomolecular Research (Donnelly

Thermodynamics Building

CCBR). Rosebrugh's west facade is still fully exposed, but its east facade is now incorporated into the Donnelly CCBR's atrium. Both facades display grandly arched windows and sophisticated brickwork.

Although the structure is largely embedded in the dense built fabric of the southeast campus precinct, it is still possible to grasp the extraordinary talent of Frank Darling, the primary designer of the building.

17g. Mechanical Engineering Building
Thermodynamics Building *Darling & Pearson, 1909*
New (west) building *Allward & Gouinlock Architects, 1948*

Darling & Pearson's original design for the Thermodynamics Building was ambitious, consisting of a laboratory wing running east-west and a taller, more imposing office and classroom wing facing west, fronting on King's College Road; due to budgetary problems in 1908, only the laboratory wing, which is now part of the Mechanical Engineering complex, was completed. The north face of this wing features a handsome doorway composition, with fine stonework rising to an elegant pediment. The wing's seven rhythmic brick arches are brought into magnificent relief when late afternoon sun strikes them from the northwest. Embedded in the old Thermodynamics Building was a boiler plant, vented by a pair of tall brick chimneys that are joined at the top. Although largely hidden today by new buildings, it is worth the effort to find these sculpturally captivating elements.

Mechanical Engineering Building (west building)

After World War Two, funding was available to complete the missing wing along King's College Road. The new, functionalist Mechanical Engineering Building opened in 1948. Designed by Allward & Gouinlock Architects, it is one of Toronto's most significant mid-twentieth-century modern buildings, showing influences from both the German Bauhaus school and the Dutch de Stijl movement.

The limestone-clad building's classrooms, shops, laboratories, offices, and lecture theaters are efficiently distributed within a simple rectangular plan. An austere stair, rising near the entry and incorporating vertical corner glazing and an elegant stainless steel clock, divides the west-facing facade into two parts. The larger, left part features three horizontal-band windows, while the right part has one at the top of an otherwise blank wall. This upper band continues at the south elevation and wraps around the east face. A wonderful two-story steel casement window with a slightly projecting balcony graces the south elevation.

Behind the Mechanical Engineering wing is a tight web of alleylike service spaces between the Haultain, Rosebrugh, and Mining buildings. Here, in a compact secretive zone, one can quietly feast on architectural history.

18. Cumberland House *Frederic Cumberland, 1860*
Renovations *William Storm, 1883*

This historically and architecturally important house at 33 St. George Street provides office and meeting space for the International Student Centre. Sadly, Cumberland House has largely been stripped of its bucolic setting and is now surrounded on three sides by asphalt. Its main entrance was originally on the east, and a long lawn stretched southward to College Street. (The house turned its back to St. George Street on the west until it was remodeled in 1883. What appears today as the front yard was originally the backyard.) Today, a small fenced lawn momentarily recalls nineteenth-century Toronto.

Inside, it is still possible to enjoy the fine proportions, superb moldings, and elegant fireplaces in the principal rooms on the ground floor. The circular stained glass light above the main stair is spectacular. Amidst these few preserved spaces one can imagine how splendid the entire mansion must have been, nearly 150 years ago, when Frederic Cumberland and his family lived there.

Cumberland, who was one of Canada's most distinguished architects and an accomplished civil engineer, railway manager, and politician, was thirty-seven when he finished his house, which he called "Pendarves," in 1860, and had just completed his masterpiece, University College, the year before. How interesting to think that he could rise in the morning and gaze from the second floor, across the pasture fields filled with grazing cows and sheep, and see his other creation, University College, a thousand feet (three hundred meters) to the north.

Cumberland House

Cumberland lived at Pendarves for twenty-one years. After his death, his business partner, architect William Storm, remodeled the house for A. Morgan Cosby. Storm moved the main entrance from the east side, running the entrance hall through to a new vestibule and front door on the west. The University of Toronto purchased the house in 1921, and it served the schools of law and business before becoming a gathering place for international students in 1966. This most recent use seems quite appropriate, given that Pendarves means "meeting place" in Cornish.

WALK TWO: THE EAST CAMPUS

HOSKIN AVENUE

Walk Two: The East Campus

Although separated from the University of Toronto's central historic campus by a mere five-minute walk across Queen's Park, the east campus presents a different world: the topography is more varied, the architecture more conservative, and the pace slower. Moreover, two of the university's oldest colleges dominate this verdant part of the campus: the University of St. Michael's College (which affiliated with the University of Toronto in 1881) and Victoria University (which joined in 1890).

This rich history is underscored by the fact that the oldest building of the university is found here, St. Basil's Church (1856), which is part of St. Michael's College. Commanding a hilltop, stoic St. Basil's overlooks Bay Street and bears silent witness to the intense real estate development that has burst forth along this street during the past four decades. Generic modern high-rise apartment towers, hotels, and office blocks line the north-south thoroughfare cheek by jowl. Another urban layer is about to be added here, because, in order to generate needed revenue, St. Michael's College sold a major parcel to a developer that will construct two residential high-rise towers and a group of town houses just north of St. Basil's Church. The peaceful inner sanctum of St. Basil's will still be there, but the church's gentle yet commanding presence in the cityscape will be greatly reduced. A portion of the university's distinctive easternmost edge will also be erased, allowing the infiltration of Bay Street commercialism and the curious mingling of the sacred and the profane.

The story of the changing east campus goes beyond St. Michael's: Victoria University has similarly sold land recently, one piece slated for a twenty-three-story condominium on Charles Street West at the northeast corner of "Vic," as the university is known. The ringing and infiltration of the University of Toronto campus with condominium towers has called forth varying opinions; some find this dynamic flowing together of town and gown a positive change while others regard it as the development of an ambiguous "cultural soup." But even with these dramatic changes, the east campus will continue to be a distinctive part of the university and the city.

19. Victoria University

Victoria University evolved from the Wesleyan Methodists' Upper Canada Academy, located in Cobourg, Ontario, 68 miles (110 kilometers) east of Toronto. The academy changed its name to Victoria College in 1841 and became Victoria University in 1884. During the late 1880s, it went through a complex process of affiliation with the University of Toronto, left Cobourg, and commenced construction of a grand new building at the northeast corner of Queen's Park. Today Victoria University

Victoria College

consists of Victoria College, a nondenominational arts and science college, and Emmanuel College, a United Church theological college. Together they support more than 3,500 students.

Vic's campus is roughly divided into two halves by Charles Street West, with the main quadrangle, centered by Victoria College, located in the southern half. Following allocation of land for the new building in 1886, the university held a limited architectural competition, in which four firms participated. Langley & Burke's proposal was deemed "most attractive," but the selection committee found some of the internal planning unsuitable, and the firm was eventually replaced by architect Willam Storm, a former Vic student.

Storm put forward various designs, including a "Proposed Grouped Design" consisting of three buildings—the Main Building, the Residence Hall, and the Gymnasium—forming a quadrangle, an idea that might also have stemmed from

Nathaniel Burwash, who was president when Vic moved from Cobourg to Toronto and had taken a trip in the summer of 1888 to the United States to study and gain ideas from campuses and new college buildings there. Only the Main Building (Victoria College) was eventually realized (see page 18). The Vic quadrangle as it exists today is a mature composition of buildings and spaces anchored by Storm's sculptural essay of 1892. Traditional and modern buildings coexist, balancing formality and informality.

19a. Victoria College *William Storm, 1892*

Work on Victoria College began in January 1891 and, although the building was not completely finished, it opened in October 1892, providing accommodation for administration, classrooms, a chapel, library, and students' and professors' rooms. The entire cost of Victoria College, including furnishings, landscaping, and fencing, amounted to $212,000.

Victoria College is a powerful edifice, commanding a gentle hill at the north end of Queen's Park. Designed by Storm in the Romanesque style developed by Henry Hobson Richardson in the United States (defined by his 1877 Trinity Church in Boston), it is a strong object-building while simultaneously playing an important role in urban space making. Its monumental presence centers the main Victoria University quadrangle but also breaks that urban space into two smaller, comfortably scaled zones.

The building itself displays all of the characteristics of the highly integrated Richardsonian Romanesque style: massive stonework, large semicircular arches, expressive towers and turrets, and colorful decorative patterning. Storm's asymmetrical composition of the grand south portal and main tower are particularly striking, achieving both balance and tension. This was the last work of the artistic William Storm, who died on August 8, 1892, two months before the new Victoria College opened.

19b. Burwash Hall *Sproatt & Rolph, 1912*
Upper Burwash House *1913*
Lower Burwash House *1931*

When the new Victoria College was conceived, both President Burwash and architect William Storm called for a group of buildings, but only one was realized. In 1903 Annesley Hall was completed on a separate plot of land to the north, but two decades passed before the additional structures imagined by Burwash and Storm for the central Victoria campus appeared: the Birge-Carnegie Library in 1910 and

Burwash Hall

Burwash Hall and Residences (now Burwash Hall and Upper Burwash House) in 1912/13. With the addition of Emmanuel College and the Emmanuel College Residence (now Lower Burwash House) in 1931, based on Sproatt & Rolph's master plan of 1928/29, the semblance of a quadrangle developed that would later be completed by the addition of the E. J. Pratt Library, Northrop Frye Hall, and the Isabel Bader Theatre.

Burwash Hall and what is now Upper Burwash House were made possible through a gift from the Massey Estate, and Chester Massey took great interest in the design, having in view no ordinary building for the one hundred male students that it would accommodate. Sproatt & Rolph, who would conceive the magnificent Hart House student union for the University of Toronto a few years later, designed the linked Burwash dining hall and residence in the collegiate Gothic style, forming an L and giving meaningful definition to the main Vic quadrangle. The residence hall consists of four houses in the English college manner, each with an entrance onto the quad. The dining hall, which features six huge Gothic windows on both the north and south facades, seats 260 students at sixteen large tables. Hanging on the western wall is Queen Victoria's burial flag, given to Vic soon after the queen's death.

In 1931 an L-shaped residential wing was added to the south for Emmanuel College, the theological division of Victoria University. Also designed by Sproatt & Rolph, it continued the collegiate Gothic vocabulary of gray Credit Valley rubble stone with Indiana limestone trim and high-pitched roofs finished in green slate. Similar to the organization of the 1913 residence to the north, Lower Burwash House has five houses.

A walkway along the west side of the building, which is built into a slope, steps down to the south and passes alongside the Lester B. Pearson Garden for Peace and Understanding adjacent to the E. J. Pratt Library. Walking from Charles Street along Upper and Lower Burwash houses down to Queen's Park is one of the most rewarding spatial experiences offered on the east campus.

19c. Birge-Carnegie Library *Sproatt & Rolph, 1910*
Emmanuel College *1931*

Birge Carnegie Library

Although today they appear to be one continuous structure, the Birge-Carnegie Library at the north and Emmanuel College to the south were constructed separately, the former finished in 1910, the latter in 1931. Together they face the northern extension of Queen's Park Crescent (Avenue Road) and form the western side of the Victoria University quadrangle.

In 1906, following Vic's request for funding, Pittsburgh industrialist Andrew Carnegie agreed to allocate $50,000 for a new library if the institution could match these funds with an endowment for permanent maintenance. A wealthy Vic alumnus, Cyrus Birge, agreed to do so in 1907, and the university launched a design competition in 1908, inviting three of Toronto's leading firms to compete: George M. Miller (who had completed Annesley Hall in 1903), Burke and Horwood, and Sproatt & Rolph. The winning design by Sproatt & Rolph was a collegiate Gothic building organized into a cruciform plan.

Constructed of Georgetown gray, Credit Valley ashlar with Indiana limestone trim, the building's primary axis runs north-south, with the main entrance at the north end. The soaring Men's Reading Room occupied the west wing. A secondary entrance facing Queen's Park is surmounted by a large statue of Queen Victoria made of Bath Stone by the Bromsgrove Guild of Worcestershire, England. The Birge-Carnegie building served as Vic's main library until 1960, when the E. J. Pratt Library was opened. (In recent years, the Birge-Carnegie Library housed the United Church of Canada's archives and the Victoria University archives.)

In 1928/29 Sproatt & Rolph developed a comprehensive master plan to "provide buildings for the new Emmanuel on the grounds of Victoria." This included an administration/library/classroom building, student residences, and a chapel for Emmanuel College, all designed in the collegiate Gothic style and adding strong urban edges to the emerging Vic quadrangle. As part of their vision, Sproatt & Rolph made preliminary drawings for what would have been an astonishing chapel at the northeast corner of Queen's Park. Due to the Great Depression, only parts of the master plan were eventually realized.

In 1931 the Emmanuel College building was added to the south end of the Birge-Carnegie Library, incorporating a much more modest chapel than originally proposed. Faced in the same Credit Valley stone as the library, the college has hidden roofs and longer, lower lines that make it appear more modern than the abutting building. The second-story Emmanuel College Library is especially splendid with large, perpendicular tracery windows facing west. Walls of Indiana limestone meet a handsome floor made of inlaid travertine terrazzo, and a massive fireplace anchors the south end of the room. Arcades along the east side frame eight mezzanine study alcoves. A family of eight beautifully crafted wrought-iron chandeliers bring sparkle to this magnificent space.

To the north of Birge-Carnegie Library and Emmanuel College is the Korean Pagoda Garden, which honors Dr. Sang Chul Lee, Chancellor of Victoria University from 1992 to 1998. At the center of the garden is a stone monument constructed in the Republic of Korea, given by the alumni of Yonsei University College of Medicine to commemorate three early Canadian Medical Missionaries that served people on the Korean peninsula.

19d. E. J. Pratt Library *Gordon Adamson & Associates, 1960*
Renovation *Shore Tilbe Irwin and Partners with Kohn Shnier Architects, 2004*

Originally called the Victoria College Library, the building was renamed in 1967 to honor the poet E. J. Pratt. Austere and minimal on the exterior, the library recently underwent an interior renovation that moved it into the twenty-first century. The new spaces created by Martin Kohn and John Shnier are carefully proportioned and enlivened with pattern and color. Rows of large white ceiling discs hover overhead; dramatic red walls appear; and venturing up the light-drenched central stair becomes an event—a climb rewarded at the top by the display of an ornate chair that belonged to Sir John Graves Simcoe, first Lieutenant Governor of Upper Canada from 1791 to 1796.

Built into the slope that rises to Victoria College, the library's lower floor has continuous glazing on three sides. The east side overlooks the restful Lester B. Pearson Garden for Peace and Understanding, designed by landscape architect Paul Ehnes. Pearson, a 1919 Vic graduate, was chancellor from 1952 to 1959 and

TOP: *E. J. Pratt Library*

BOTTOM: *E. J. Pratt Library, interior*

Isabel Bader Theater

Canada's fourteenth prime minister. He helped define Canada's modern foreign policy and was awarded the Nobel Peace Prize in 1957.

Seven years after the E. J. Pratt Library was finished, Northrop Frye Hall was completed to the west. Designed by Gordon Adamson & Associates, it pairs with the library to make a set of "bookend blocks" that frame the south approach to Victoria University.

19e. Isabel Bader Theatre *Lett/Smith Architects, 2001*

This understated, dignified building faces Charles Street, filling a gap that existed along the north edge of Vic's main quadrangle. Interestingly, it roughly achieves what President Burwash had imagined a hundred years earlier when he called for "the library and residence meeting in the north to form a quadrangle opening to the sunny south."

Constructed of exposed concrete, Owen Sound limestone, stucco, and wood, the theater's cubic forms blend easily with the Birge-Carnegie Library to the west and Burwash Hall to the east. The acoustically superb five-hundred-seat auditorium is used for plays and film screenings, and as a general-purpose classroom. The building resulted from a large donation from Alfred Bader, given to honor his wife Isabel, a Victoria alumna.

19f. Annesley Hall
George M. Miller, 1903

Annesley Hall

When the industrialist Hart Almerrin Massey died in 1896, he made provision in his will for the construction of a women's residence at Vic, and in 1897 the Women's Educational Association was formed to make it happen. The new residence designed by George M. Miller opened in October 1903, providing forty-eight rooms along with a dining room, gymnasium, and infirmary. The building was named for Susanna Annesley, the mother of the early leader of the Methodist movement, John Wesley.

Annesley Hall's Jacobethan-revival design merges the Jacobean and Elizabethan styles that were popular in nineteenth-century England. Miller imaginatively combined fancy, curved, front-facing gables (which are also Dutch-influenced), elaborate chimneys, and rectangular windows with small leaded panes to create this lovely residence, intended at the turn of the twentieth century to be "a home of high moral tone in an atmosphere of refined social culture."

19g. Wymilwood *Fleury & Arthur, 1953*
Addition *Moriyama & Teshima Architects, 2010*

The story of Wymilwood, Vic's modernist student union, is fascinating. In 1925 Mrs. Edward R. Wood donated her Queen's Park mansion, called Wymilwood, to Vic as a center for female students, and it served that role until 1953, when the new coeducational student union opened one block to the east. The mansion was subsequently named Falconer Hall in 1952 and is now part of the Faculty of Law (see page 131). The name Wymilwood was transferred to the new student union, and gateposts from the mansion (without their original stone spheres on top) can be seen in front of the union.

One of the building's authors, Eric Arthur, was then professor of architecture at the University of Toronto, well known as both a preservationist and promoter of progressive architecture. In the case of Victoria University, it seems that Arthur was not wearing his preservationist hat. He and his firm partner William Fleury launched a master plan for Vic in 1950 that emphasized athletic fields, parking lots, and new

Wymilwood

dormitories—a scheme that called for the eventual demolishing of two magnificent historic structures: the central Victoria College building and the architecturally intriguing Annesley Hall.

The construction of a new student union—Wymilwood—was central to Fleury & Arthur's radical approach and formed stage one of their master plan. Stage two was the addition of an angular, three-hundred-seat auditorium attached to the west, and stage three called for a large L-shaped dormitory atop and extending north and east from the cafeteria, requiring the tearing down of historic Annesley Hall. (This unrealized master plan explains why Wymilwood is awkwardly connected to Annesley Hall. It was supposed to be a temporary arrangement.) Thankfully, the central Victoria College building and Annesley Hall were spared the wrecking ball. Only the student union and Margaret Addison Hall, a semblance of the dormitory proposed in the master plan, were built.

When it opened in 1953, Wymilwood was a spirited modernist work, offering a gentle, domestic-scaled environment conducive to student life. Fleury & Arthur set the building back from Charles Street to create a sunken, south-facing terrace extending from a coffee shop. On the upper floors, common rooms, a reading room, and music room were carefully detailed and included period lighting fixtures from Canada, Denmark, England, Italy, Sweden, and the United States. The folded-plate roof over the cafeteria was also of the period and continues to give the building a light, airy feeling, even though the insertion of faculty offices has compromised this wing.

Some key interior features of this important Toronto modern building have been neglected in recent years. However, the basic bones remain, including the elegant main stair, a spiral of reinforced concrete supported on a semicircular masonry wall. As a social union, Wymilwood can no longer fulfill all the needs of today's students, and Vic has commenced a major addition by Moriyama & Teshima Architects that respects but avoids slavishly imitating the original building—an approach that would surely have pleased Arthur.

19h. Margaret Addison Hall
Gordon Adamson & Associates, 1959

Margaret Addison Hall

In the late 1950s, as a result of the post–World War Two baby boom and increasing enrollment of women, Vic needed more residence space. Fleury & Arthur's 1950 master plan had called for a new L-shaped dormitory north of Charles Street, integrated with Wymilwood. Margaret Addison Hall seems to have evolved from that vision, even though it is located further to the northeast and stands alone.

Named after the university's first dean of women, the six-story, boomerang-shaped building included sixty double rooms and eighty single rooms for women, along with music and typing rooms and a room in the basement for storing evening dresses and crinolines. Its main floor included a suave, cylindrical, wood-panelled library. The residence hall was affectionately referred to as "six stories of glory with a twist in the middle."

Now coeducational, most of the building's glory has faded, and the forecourt that Margaret Addison Hall shares with Wymilwood is run down. Moriyama & Teshima Architects' addition to the student union will reshape and revitalize this open space.

19i. Rowell Jackman Hall
Keith Becker Architects with Kuwabara Payne McKenna Blumberg Architects, 1993

Situated between Charles Street West and St. Mary Street at the easternmost edge of the Vic campus, Rowell Jackman Hall is an apartment-style coeducational residence. The primary six-story volume is clad in oversized orange bricks; three more stories are stepped back and clad in neutral brown steel panels. This stepped configuration and material application generate a background building that responds to and respects the scale of its urban context.

Lillian Massey Department of Household Science

19j. Lillian Massey Department of Household Science
George M. Miller, 1912

Although the title gracing the west-facing portico indicates otherwise, this outstanding building owned by Victoria University is no longer the home of courses in
the domestic sciences for women. The south half houses the University of Toronto's
Department of Classics, Centre for Mediaeval Studies, and other academic divisions, while the north half is leased by the clothing retailer Club Monaco.

Known first as the School of Household Science, the building was sponsored
by Lillian Massey Treble, a daughter of Hart Massey (after whom Hart House would
later be named). Degrees in household science were first offered by the university
in 1902. Massey Treble contributed half a million dollars toward the building, which
Miller designed in the classical tradition, appropriately employing the feminine Ionic
order. The building's main facade fronting the Royal Ontario Museum is templelike
with four Ionic columns, bracketed to the left and right by sets of three engaged
columns. The secondary north facade (now the entrance to Club Monaco) has four
engaged Ionic columns between pedimented end pieces.

The building's main, marble-faced stair hall is worth visiting. It presents fine pre-
Raphaelite stained-glass windows showing women tending to household tasks and
men hunting and harvesting.

McKinsey Building

19k. McKinsey Building
Taylor Hariri Pontarini Architects, 1999

Constructed on land owned by Victoria University (with a future option for Vic to take over the building for academic purposes), this three-story structure houses the Canadian headquarters of McKinsey & Company, an international consulting firm. Taylor Hariri Pontarini Architects took a holistic approach and engaged in an unusually large agenda for the 75,000-square-foot project (6,970 square meters)—conducting research on the workplace, urban design, architecture, landscape, interior design, and furniture design—leading to a rigorous resolution that makes it one of the most admired places in downtown Toronto.

The zig-zag floor plan responds to the immediate urban conditions. At the south the building is tight to the street and offers an elegant canopy, while on the west it embraces a courtyard that overlooks the Vic playing field. The east edge is intentionally less adventurous, facing toward a new condominium tower and accommodating a ramp down to the parking level. The north end of the building has a secondary entrance from Sultan Street.

Taking cues from the many stone-clad buildings at Victoria University (and further south, at St. Michael's College), the McKinsey Building features gray Owen Sound stone, rough-cut for the ground floor and smooth-cut for the upper two floors. Set into the stone walls are generously sized windows with frames made of mahogany and operable ventilation units. The large areas of glazing bring natural light deep into the working environment. The heart of the building is a three-story informal meeting place called "the hive." Here and throughout the project there is a sense of warmth, provided by fireplaces, marble counters, Oriental rugs, and cherry wood furniture—a kind of collective "big house."

20. The University of St. Michael's College

Founded in 1852 as a Roman Catholic boys' school, which by 1853 functioned under the Basilian Fathers as a high school, *college classique,* and minor seminary, St. Michael's College has been at its current location on Clover Hill since 1856. Today it has more than 4,200 full-time students and is the largest Catholic post-secondary educational institution in English-speaking Canada. Its graduate Faculty of Theology is one of the largest theology schools in North America.

The tight cluster of fifteen buildings constituting St. Michael's stretches from Queen's Park to Bay Street, merging at the college's northwest corner with Victoria University and at its southwest corner with St. Regis College, part of the Toronto School of Theology. It is an architecturally diverse campus, employing a broad range of building materials, such as limestone, copper, yellow brick, red brick, and concrete. To some extent the rolling, terraced, wooded landscape holds this mélange of styles and materials together. Only one vehicular route, St. Joseph Street, cuts through the minicampus, allowing pedestrians and bicycles to prevail.

20a. St. Basil's Church and Odette Hall *William Hay, 1856*
Southeast wing *William T. Thomas, 1862*
North extension *architect unknown, 1878*
Southern extension and tower *A. A. Post, 1887*
Steeple and spire *Arthur W. Holmes, 1895*
Odette Hall renovations *Carlos Ott Partnership, 1996*

In 1853 Captain John Elmsley, owner of the country estate Clover Hill, donated four lots to the Basilian fathers on the condition they build a parish church; later that year the Basilians purchased four additional lots from him, reflecting their grander aspirations. Architect William Hay proposed a large complex of Gothic-style buildings around a quadrangle, including St. Basil's Church. It was a complete, picturesque vision, set amidst pastures and wooded hills (see page 17). Tenders were let for the church and one wing of the college, and both opened in 1856. The parish was growing rapidly, however, and within a year more space was needed.

Hay's total vision was never realized. Instead, the church and college proceeded to expand piecemeal, with work completed by numerous architects over a sixty-six-year period. A southeast addition to the college wing opened in 1862; together with the original wing it is now known as Odette Hall, named in honor of art patron Louis L. Odette. It was recently renovated to display the college's extensive collection of modern religious art.

The college undertook large extensions in 1873 and 1903 (both demolished in 1971). In 1878 the original five-sided apse of the church was demolished, and the

St. Basil's Church and Sam Sorbara Hall (left)

sanctuary was extended fifty feet (15.2 meters) to the northeast; a new entrance, narthex, and tower were added in 1887; and in 1895 a slate-covered steeple and spire were completed (replaced with copper in the 1950s). In 1922 a plaster vaulted ceiling was installed in the sanctuary.

Despite this topsy-turvy history, St. Basil's has miraculously survived and remains as a beautiful, solemn place of worship in Toronto's downtown. After he died in 1863, Captain John Elmsley's body was buried in St. Michael's Cathedral; but his heart was buried separately, per his request, in the west wall of St. Basil's, marked by a white marble plaque. One must wonder what he would make of the continuing and complex sequence of building up and tearing down that has gone on for more than 150 years on his beloved Clover Hill.

20b. Brennan Hall *Arthur W. Holmes, 1937*
Addition and renovation *Brennan & Whale, 1968*

Brennan Hall

Brennan Hall, St. Michael's central common space, was the second building at the college by architect Arthur W. Holmes. An accomplished ecclesiastical architect, Holmes trained in the office of the prominent London, England architect George E. Street and, after arriving in Toronto in 1886, devoted virtually all of his career to serving the Roman Catholic church in the Toronto region.

For Brennan Hall, Holmes again used Credit Valley limestone with robust patterns and textures, which he had used so effectively two years earlier for Teefy Hall and the Pontifical Institute of Medieval Studies. The main entrance to Brennan Hall is on axis with Elmsley Place, and an attractive dining hall is located east of the entrance on the second floor.

A major addition by Brennan & Whale in 1968, set at a forty-five-degree angle with the original building, feels awkward and unresolved.

20c. Elmsley Hall *Brennan & Whale, 1955*

Elmsley Hall

This midcentury men's residence hall has a low wing facing St. Mary Street and a five-story main wing running south, terminated by a cubic power plant. Here at the south end, the architecture becomes richer, with the power plant and its chimney, a pedestrian underpass beneath a vehicular service bridge, and a series of south-facing, terraced flower gardens forming an interesting composition. The slightly concave south face of the bridge-underpass further underscores the subtle relationships among the building components and the landscape.

Elmsley Hall and the attached power plant are faced in Credit Valley limestone—from rough-cut to striated to smooth—which was the dominant building material at St. Michael's from the 1930s through the 1950s.

20d. Elmsley Place

Bellisle House, 1 Elmsley Place
Langley & Langley, 1896
Addition *J. P. Hynes, 1910*

McCorkell House, 2 Elmsley Place *(joined to Sullivan House, 96 St. Joseph Street, 1890s)*
M. B. Aylesworth, 1892
Additions *Burke, Horwood & White, 1897, 1903*

Phelan House, 3 Elmsley Place
Langley & Langley, 1897

Windle House, 5 Elmsley Place
Attributed to John M. Lyle, 1897

Gilson-Maritain House, 6–8 Elmsley Place
A. Frank Wickson, 1901

Elmsley Place

One-block-long Elmsley Place—an enclave of historic houses serving as administrative offices and residences for faculty and students—is a charming world of its own. The plan for this minisubdivision—Toronto's first subdivision—was registered in 1890 by Remigius Elmsley, son of Captain John Elmsley, who in 1853 had donated land from his Clover Hill estate for St. Michael's College and St. Basil's Church. Remigius Elmsley's own house, built in the 1870s, originally stood northwest of where Brennan Hall stands today. Between 1892 and 1901 a street called Elmsley Place was created, and six large fashionable houses were built on "villa lots," five of which remain. (Willison House was demolished in 1962.)

The houses are all constructed of red brick, but their architectural styles vary. From 2007 to 2008, the firm of Goldsmith Borgal completed extensive preservation and restoration work on the houses along the west side of Elmsley Place, and thoughtful landscaping complements this impressive project.

Teefy Hall and the Pontifical Institute of Mediaeval Studies

20e. Teefy Hall and the Pontifical Institute of Mediaeval Studies *Arthur W. Holmes, 1936*

An architectural drawing by Arthur W. Holmes, published in 1929, shows a proposal for a long continuous building in the collegiate Gothic style facing Queen's Park and stretching from Victoria University at the north to St. Joseph Street at the south. Presumably because of the Great Depression, the extraordinary project was not realized. Instead, in 1936, St. Michael's College completed this pleasing building, which includes residences for men—the More, Fisher, and Teefy houses—along with the prestigious Pontifical Institute of Mediaeval Studies, founded in 1929.

Carr Hall

Wings of the U-shaped stone structure extend toward Queen's Park, forming a lovely forecourt, from which a covered passageway leads to a peaceful quadrangle behind the building. The Credit Valley limestone that Holmes specified for the building is noteworthy because it was the first use of this material at St. Michael's College. (Five buildings were clad in this type of stone in the nineteen-year period between 1935 and 1954.) It presents an array of wonderful patterns and textures, inviting close examination and touch, and we can sense the great craftsmanship it required. There is something appropriately suggestive of "the mediaeval" here, and it seems regrettable that this material vocabulary was not continued after 1954.

20f. Carr Hall *Ernest Cormier with Brennan & Whale, 1954*

Carr Hall, a classroom and office facility, is the third building completed for St. Michael's College by the highly regarded Montreal-based architect Ernest Cormier. It has a prominent location at the northeast corner of Queen's Park Crescent East and St. Joseph Street, forming a quadrangle with Teefy Hall and the houses on the west side of Elmsley Place.

Named for Father Henry Carr, a leader of Roman Catholic religious education in Canada and cofounder, with Professor Etienne Gilson, of the Pontifical Institute of Mediaeval Studies, the building is modest, even austere; there are some surprises, though, including the abstract west facade, which has a grid of square windows, and the sculpturally inventive tower. The patterned, textured stone is nearly identical to that of neighboring Teefy Hall. While Carr Hall is essentially modern in style, it sits comfortably with the much older buildings around it.

LEFT: *Carr Hall, west facade*
RIGHT: *Sam Sorbara Hall*

20g. Sam Sorbara Hall *Carlos Ott Partnership, 2001*

Thirty-two years passed between the completion of the John M. Kelly Library
in 1969 and the opening of St. Michael's College's next building project, Sam
Sorbara Hall in 2001, resulting in a lot of speculation among the university community about what design direction St. Michael's would take after the three-decade lull
in construction.

The site selected for the new men's residence was a particularly difficult one on
the south slope of Clover Hill, a stone's throw from the historic St. Basil's Church
and Odette Hall. The site was also adjacent to three historic houses on Elmsley
Place. The college opted for an historicist approach: the postmodern Sorbara Hall
mimics characteristics of St. Basil's and Odette Hall with its yellow brick, steeply
sloped roofs, and dormer windows. Unlike the 1950s Cormier-designed buildings
at St. Michael's, which fused contextual considerations with spare, utilitarian modernism (and in the case of Carr Hall, considerable formal invention), the overt, thin
historicism of Sam Sorbara Hall is disappointing. Although it appropriately defers
to St. Basil's Church, it lacks the kind of deeper resonance and criticality that could
have brought the architecture of Sam Sorbara Hall and St. Michael's College into
the twenty-first century.

20h. Cardinal Flahiff Basilian Centre
Ernest Cormier with Brennan & Whale, 1949
Addition *Brennan & Whale, 1959*
Addition and alterations *John J. Farrugia, 1979*

During the late 1940s and early 1950s, St. Michael's College engaged Ernest
Cormier to design three buildings: a boys' school, St. Basil's Seminary (now
the Cardinal Flahiff Basilian Centre), and Carr Hall. The school, completed in
1948, was located at the edge of the city's tony Forest Hill neighborhood and

LEFT: *Cardinal Flahiff Basilian Centre*
RIGHT: *John M. Kelly Library*

employed materials and elements found in Cormier's masterwork, the main pavilion of the University of Montreal (1924–43). The boys' school's distinctive tower is strongly reminiscent of the imposing tower above the entrance of the University of Montreal's main pavilion.

Immediately following the boys' school, Cormier completed St. Basil's Seminary on the college's main campus. E-shaped in plan, the design is typical of Cormier's calm, careful modernism, incorporating yellow brick and handsome stone detailing. The center wing of the "E" houses a simple chapel, stacked above a dining hall. Although spare and utilitarian—the interior walls are unadorned concrete block with simple color banding—the chapel has thoughtful touches such as a patterned terrazzo floor.

In 1979 the front of the seminary was drastically altered. The heavy-looking concrete addition and accompanying piers are unfortunate, serving as a reminder of the less appealing aspects of 1960s/70s Brutalism, when some architects misunderstood and misapplied Corbusian notions.

20i. John M. Kelly Library *John J. Farrugia, 1969*

During the 1960s and 1970s, many architects ran wild with the structural, sculptural, and textural possibilities of reinforced concrete, and the John M. Kelly Library is an aggressive example. Architect John J. Farrugia constructed the floor plates of what is known as "two-way waffle slabs," which are exposed in the lobby ceiling. The battered concrete walls on the eastern part of the building's base have a ridged, highly textured surface—the "corduroy" kind that one critic recently referred to as "delightfully horrifying." Above the battered wall is a three-story zone of "concrete hoods" that contain windows and catch the sunlight in dramatic ways. Indeed, the John M. Kelly Library is a *tour de force*, and visitors should examine it not just from the front on St. Joseph Street but on all sides, including the rear laneway elevation.

Muzzo Family Almni Hall and John M. Kelley Library (left)

20j. Muzzo Family Alumni Hall *Mathers & Haldenby, 1930, 1946*
Renovations *John J. Farrugia, 1983*

The Muzzo Family Alumni Hall was originally a two-story structure housing the
Ontario Research Foundation Laboratories; two floors were added in 1946.
Although Alumni Hall is an unobtrusive building that is easy to pass by, its hybrid
design—with one foot in the classical tradition and another stepping into modernism—is worth a second look. The long east elevation, which is rhythmically marked
by fluted but abstracted two-story pilasters, is the most attractive. The "square-
within-square" spandrel panels between the windows are made of Monel metal, a
material that became popular during the streamlined modern era of the late 1920s
to the early 1950s.

LEFT: *Toronto School of Theology*
RIGHT: *St. Regis College*

21. The Mansions on Queen's Park Crescent East

Toronto's Queen's Park was opened by the Prince of Wales in 1861, and soon the adjacent region to the east became a fashionable area for the city's establishment to build town villas. Formidable brick houses in the latest architectural styles, with elegant coach houses behind, lined Queen's Park Crescent East. In 1981 the Province of Ontario transferred most of the properties on the east side of Queen's Park, between Wellesley Street West and St. Joseph Street, to the University of Toronto. Fortunately, most of these mansions have been preserved and now serve various academic purposes.

21a. 47 Queen's Park Crescent East: Toronto School of Theology *David B. Dick, 1892*
Additions *Curry, Sproatt & Rolph, 1906*
Renovations *Moffat Kinoshita Partnership, 1983*

Exuberant and full of verve, this house was built for Reuben Millichamp, partner in Millichamp, Coyle & Co., wholesale distributors of cloth, blankets, and furs. The complex, rhythmic integration of architectural components is impressive, from the sophisticated manner in which the house turns the southeast corner to the charm of small details such as the terra-cotta panel of Hollyhocks above the front door, to the left.

In 1921 the property was acquired by the province and housed the Ontario Railway and Municipal Board, and in 1929 the Ontario Research Foundation occupied the house. Following renovations in 1983, it became the home of the Toronto School of Theology (TST) which is affiliated with the university. The TST, with its

LEFT: *Faculty of Law*
RIGHT: *Christie Mansion (Regis College)*

seven member schools, is the largest ecumenical center for theological education in the English-speaking world.

21b. 43 Queen's Park Crescent East: St. Regis College

Beaumont Jarvis, 1896
Coach house and stable *attributed to George W. Gouinlock, 1903*
Renovations *Larkin Architect Limited, 2009*

This late-Victorian mansion has an ornate oriel bay window and a bargeboard with distinctive geometric tracery. The house was commissioned by Lt. Colonel James Mason, who participated in the Fenian Raids and the North West Rebellion and, after military service, became a banker and manager of the Home Savings & Loan Corporation. In 1918, ownership passed to Colonel H. D. Lockhart Gordon. The Multicultural History Society of Ontario occupied the house from 1980 to 2007, and it has recently been leased by the University of Toronto to Regis College, which is renovating the house for academic uses.

21c. 39 Queen's Park Crescent East: Faculty of Law

George W. Gouinlock, 1903; porte cochere, 1912

This house, constructed for Sir William T. White, general manager of the National Trust Company, abounds with architectural details, from the five brick chimneys thrusting skyward to the scalloped sea shell at the central dormer. The front hall contains a fireplace with a finely crafted oak mantle and surround. Until its new building is finished, the Faculty of Law is using the house as temporary office space.

21d. 39A Queen's Park Crescent East: Marshall McLuhan Centre for Culture and Technology *George W. Gouinlock, 1903*

Marshall McLuhan Centre for Culture and Technology

Once a rear service building for the mansion at 39 Queen's Park Crescent, this dilapidated coach house is the unlikely home of the world famous McLuhan Program in Culture and Technology. In the early 1960s, Marshall McLuhan was a professor in the English department at St. Michael's College and was receiving attractive offers from foreign universities. In 1963, to retain him, the presidents of the University of Toronto and St. Michael's College created the Centre for Culture and Technology as a base for McLuhan's research. They developed ambitious plans for a new building to house the center but could not find sufficient funding. McLuhan's comment was: "We shall concentrate upon achieving an intellectual identity rather than a physical one," and the center moved into the former coach house in 1968.

Marshall McLuhan died in 1980, but his legacy and work have been carried on by the McLuhan Program in Culture and Technology, which became part of the University of Toronto's Faculty of Information Studies (now Faculty of Information) in 1994. Today the program aims at using McLuhan-inspired thinking and perception tools to investigate the effects of new human processes on culture and society.

21e. 29 Queen's Park Crescent East: (Regis College) Christie Mansion *Gordon & Helliwell, 1882*
Reconstruction and Additions *Gordon & Helliwell, 1899*
Addition and alternations *Darling & Pearson, 1910*
Renovations *Larkin Architect Limited, 2009*

The first house on this corner site was completed in 1882, a decade before the Ontario Legislature Building to the southwest. It was designed by the prominent Toronto firm Gordon & Helliwell for William Mellis Christie and executed in the late-Victorian style with ornate gables and porches. Christie, who had immigrated from Scotland in 1848, was the cofounder of the extremely successful Christie, Brown and Co., makers of baked goods. In 1899 Gordon & Helliwell radically transformed and enlarged the original house (it is unclear how much of the 1882 house was actually kept), this time employing the Tudor style.

Christie's widow died in 1909, and the house was inherited by her son, Robert Christie, who commissioned Darling & Pearson to add to the house and make

90 Wellesley Street West

alterations. The result is known today as the Christie Mansion. From the imposing *porte cochère*, one enters a vestibule leading to a stunning long hall on the right with a barrel vault decorated with plaster ropes of flowers and fruit. Beyond are other handsome rooms, including the south-facing solarium by Darling & Pearson. Robert Christie lived there with his family until his death in 1926. In his will, he left the sale of the mansion to the discretion of his trustees, who sold it to Leonard Smith who, four months later, sold it to the Sisters of St. Joseph. They then converted it to a residence for female students and in later years linked it to buildings they constructed to the east at 90 Wellesley Street West. In 2008 the University of Toronto purchased the property and leased it to Regis College, a member of the Toronto School of Theology. Regis College is converting the former mansion into a classroom, study, and office facility while retaining its architectural grandeur.

22. 90 Wellesley Street West *Gordon Adamson & Associates*
Mary Hall *1954*
Fontbonne Hall *1956*

Formerly owned by the Sisters of St. Joseph, this complex of buildings was recently purchased by the University of Toronto. St. Regis College leases parts of the complex for their library and chapel, and a student lounge.

Together, the 1954 Mary Hall at the rear and the 1956 Fontbonne Hall facing Wellesley Street West form a small mid-block courtyard. The main east-west block of the 1956 portion has a thoughtfully designed pattern of windows, combining fixed and operable units. Most noteworthy in the complex is the simple chapel, which has four decorative glass windows designed by Karel Versteeg representing Faith, Hope, Charity, and the Tree of Life.

WALK THREE: THE NORTH CAMPUS

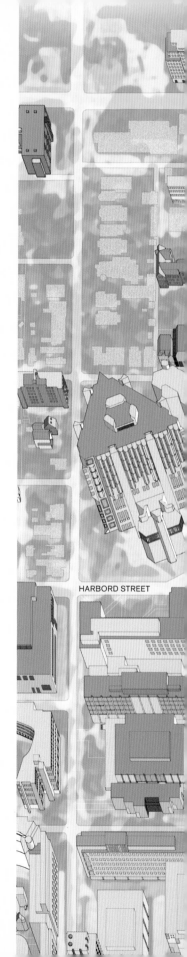

HARBORD STREET

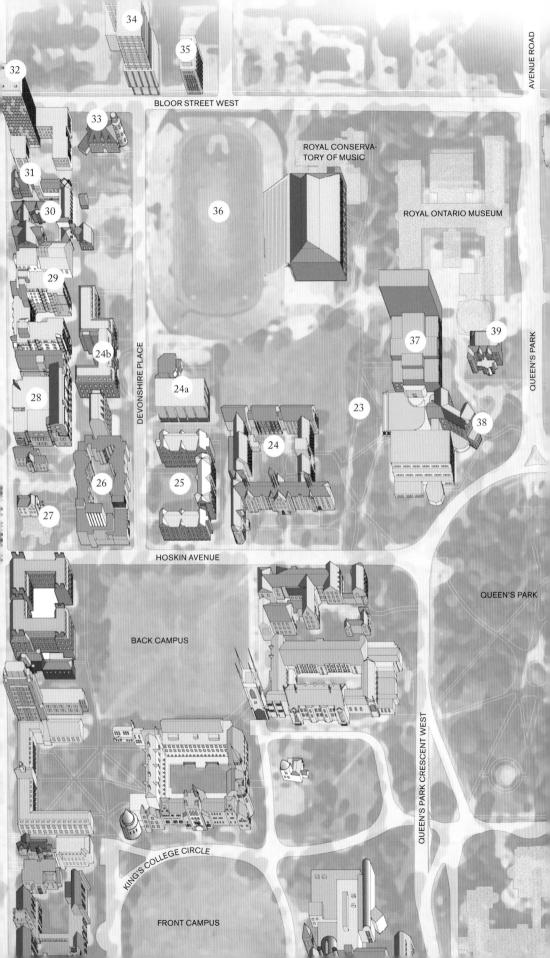

34

35

32

33

31

30

29

24b

28

24a

26

25

24

27

ROYAL CONSERVA-
TORY OF MUSIC

ROYAL ONTARIO MUSEUM

36

37

39

23

38

BLOOR STREET WEST

DEVONSHIRE PLACE

HOSKIN AVENUE

QUEEN'S PARK

AVENUE ROAD

QUEEN'S PARK

BACK CAMPUS

QUEEN'S PARK CRESCENT WEST

KING'S COLLEGE CIRCLE

FRONT CAMPUS

Walk Three: The North Campus

The north campus generally constitutes the area from Hoskin Avenue on the south to Bloor Street West on the north, and from Queen's Park (Avenue Road) on the east to St. George Street on the west. A 1923 *Goad's Atlas* map showing the University of Toronto campus reveals how underdeveloped this part of the campus used to be. The section south of Hoskin Avenue, referred to in this guide book as the historic campus (Walk One), already had some twenty-five university-owned buildings at that time, while north of Hoskin there were only six University of Toronto structures: Trinity College, three student residence buildings to the west of Trinity (now the Munk Centre for International Studies), the Dominion Meteorological Building (now Admissions and Awards), and Varsity Stadium, which had a grandstand along the west side. Both sides of St. George Street between Hoskin and Bloor were still solidly lined with private homes in 1923, but Taddle Creek was gone, its former path shown by a faint dotted line, presumably indicating what we enjoy today as Philosopher's Walk. The atlas map shows mostly open space in what is now the north campus, a reminder that this area has changed dramatically, filling in rapidly with buildings over the past eighty-five years.

Some sizeable open spaces have survived, though, and historical, social, and spatial continuity exists through the preservation and renewed use of places like Philosopher's Walk, Trinity College's playing field, and Varsity field. Even though some of the private residences along St. George were demolished and the remaining ones have been converted for institutional use, a pleasant north-south public lane now runs through what was once their backyards, linking buildings, courtyards, and quadrangles.

23. Philosopher's Walk

Landscape master plan *Michael Hough, 1962; ENVision–The Hough Group Limited, 2004*
Queen Alexandra Gateway *Chadwick & Beckett, 1901*
Bennett Gates *ENVision—The Hough Group Limited, 2006*

Shaded by a canopy of mature beech and oak trees, Philosopher's Walk winds from Bloor Street West to Hoskin Avenue through a shallow ravine through which Taddle Creek formerly flowed. This lovely meandering route is marked at the north end by the historic Queen Alexandra Gateway and at the south end by the recently constructed Bennett Gates.

Taddle Creek once ran from glacial Lake Iroquois down to the Don River and Lake Ontario, entering Toronto's harbor near what is now the city's Distillery District. Ojibway peoples fished and hunted along this route and knew the creek as "Ziibiing." With the settlement and expansion of Toronto in the eighteenth and

Bennett Gates at Philosopher's Walk

nineteenth centuries, people used Taddle Creek in new, and sometimes damaging, ways. In 1859 a dam was built to create McCaul's Pond east of University College (see page 16), and this unnatural intervention led to the stream's pollution. From the 1850s to 1870s, to deal with contamination, most of Taddle Creek was incorporated into the city's sewage system and covered over.

Interest in taming the Taddle Creek ravine can be documented as early as January 17, 1852, when the Council of King's College set aside about six acres for a botanic garden, shown in an 1852 sketch plan running southward, about one hundred yards wide, in the same location as today's Philosopher's Walk. But it was not until the early twentieth century that the walk evolved as a linear urban park, and nobody knows for certain how or when its formal name was assigned. In his 1917 "Preliminary Plan for the Landscape Improvement and General Expansion for the University of Toronto," landscape architect Bryant Fleming devoted a full page to what he referred to as the university's "valley" without ever mentioning Philosopher's Walk. A student club that existed from the 1890s to 1950s, the Philosophical Society of the University, met in the 1920s at Wymilwood (now Falconer Hall), which is located along the walk, so some speculate that this is the origin of Philosopher's Walk. Fleming recognized the potential of this distinctive part of the campus, stating in his 1917 report that

> this entire valley should be given very careful consideration, as it is one of the most important and interesting landscape features of the University grounds. It should be improved and maintained upon strictly naturalistic park lines, formality being strictly prohibited in its development, except insofar as the development of the courts and quadrangles of the adjacent buildings is concerned.

Queen Alexandra Gateway at Philosopher's Walk and Royal Ontario Museum

Fleming also called for "a good architectural entrance gateway" to the valley "between McMasters [now the Royal Conservatory of Music] and the Museum." Forty-five years passed before this was accomplished, when the Queen Alexandra Gateway was moved here in 1962. Twice relocated, the gateway originally stood at the intersection of Bloor Street West and Queen's Park (Avenue Road), marking the northern entrance to the park. It is named after Princess Alexandra Oldenburg (1844–1925), who came to England from Denmark as the wife of Edward VII, and was built to commemorate the 1901 visit of the Duke and Duchess of Cornwall and York. The lampposts, mounted atop the stone gate posts, have exquisite ironwork that serves as a fitting introduction to the naturalism of the ravine below.

In 2006 the Bennett Gates were added at the south end of Philosopher's Walk, honoring Avie Bennett, a leader in real-estate development and publishing. The huge stone pineapples that top the gateway were rescued from a gate designed by Mathers & Haldenby that formerly stood facing College Street between the 1926 FitzGerald Building and the 1932 botany greenhouses.

Philosopher's Walk continues to evolve spatially. At the north end, a major addition by Kuwabara Payne McKenna Blumberg Architects to the Royal Conservatory of Music constricts but also enlivens the transitional space into the ravine, while the crystalline Royal Ontario Museum by Daniel Libeskind adds a hovering dynamism. As the city densifies, this "fine natural valley," as Fleming called it, is increasingly treasured by Torontonians.

Trinity College

24. University of Trinity College *Darling & Pearson, 1925*
East and west wings *George & Moorhouse, 1941*
Chapel *Sir Giles Gilbert Scott, 1955*
North wing *Somerville, McMurrich and Oxley, 1961*
Quadrangle landscape *gh3 (Diana Gerrard and Pat Hanson), 2007*

Trinity College was founded in 1851 by John Strachan, the first Anglican bishop of Toronto and first president of King's College, and provided instruction in divinity, law, medicine, and the arts. The original college was located on Queen Street West, well beyond the town limits and far from the temptations of city life. Trinity federated with the University of Toronto in 1904 and opened a new building on the main campus in 1925, designed in the collegiate Gothic style by the noted architects Frank Darling and John A. Pearson. The Trinity campus now consists of the main Trinity College building facing Hoskin Avenue, the Gerald Larkin Academic Building and adjoining George Ignatieff Theatre, St. Hilda's College, and the University of Toronto's Munk Centre for International Studies, home of Trinity's John W. Graham Library. The college has 1,700 undergraduate students and some 140 students in its Faculty of Divinity, Canada's oldest Anglican theological school.

In the early 1920s, Darling & Pearson conceived of Trinity College as two quadrangles extending northward from Hoskin Avenue to what are now the Trinity

Trinity College quadrangle

playing field and the Varsity Centre. However, by 1925 only a portion along Hoskin and two short wings running northward had been completed; it took from 1941 to 1961 to finish the other three sides of the Trinity quadrangle. (The second quadrangle was never realized.) The quad is the social crossroads of Trinity College and was recently given a contemporary update by the architecture and landscape design firm gh3, who created an imaginative new carpet for the space composed of stone tracery and grass that repeats the Greek letter chi (also the character for Christ).

The Gothicized interior of Trinity College is just as spectacular as its exterior. Elegant Seeley Hall, on the second floor, was originally intended to be a reading room but was used as the college's chapel until 1955. Strachan Hall, the dining facility that forms the bulk of the west wing, includes historic portraits and a large tapestry woven in Flanders that depicts the Queen of Sheba at the court of King Solomon. A grand private residence with a baronial stair hall at the east end of the 1925 wing provides splendid quarters for Trinity's provost. But the *pièce de résistance* is the college's chapel, designed by Sir Giles Gilbert Scott, who was the architect of Liverpool Cathedral. Executed in the perpendicular-Gothic style and opened in 1955, the chapel was one of the last works by this renowned English architect. Exhilarating in its extreme verticality—the chapel soars forty-seven feet to the bosses that ornament the vaulting—the building is also remarkable for the authenticity and integrity of its traditional masonry construction. The chapel's exquisite stained glass and decorative works add to its aura, including a bronze grille in the west transept designed by Scott that leads to the Lady Chapel.

Trinity College, chapel

LEFT: *Gerald Larkin Academic Building*
RIGHT: *St. Hilda's College*

24a. Gerald Larkin Academic Building

Somerville, McMurrich and Oxley, 1961; **George Ignatieff Theatre,** *1979*

This multiuse student commons for Trinity, named for Gerald Larkin, president of the Salada Tea Company, Ltd., from 1922 to 1957, was designed by the same architects, completed in the same year, and faced in the same stone as the north wing of the neighboring Trinity College building. Its most engaging architectural feature is a covered arcade with a subtly vaulted ceiling running along its south side. Three-story-tall, closely spaced limestone fins cover the full length of the south facade, forming a screen at the arcade level. The horizontally exaggerated arcade and vertically exaggerated fins combine to create a visceral sense of the Gothic style, appropriate to Trinity.

24b. St. Hilda's College

North wing *George & Moorhouse, 1938, 1960*
South wing *Rounthwaite, Dick and Hadley Architects, 1982*

St. Hilda's College received its charter in February 1890 to provide higher education for women, in affiliation with Trinity College; in 1938, after occupying various locations around the city, it settled on Devonshire Place. During the 1920s and 1930s, the University of Toronto strongly favored, and sometimes mandated, that new buildings be Georgian in character, so it is not surprising that St. Hilda's

Munk Centre for International Studies

followed this pattern. Inside the classicized front entrance portal, a stair rises a half-level to a central foyer, which leads to Cartwright Hall, now used for lectures. It was originally St. Hilda's theater before the George Ignatieff Theatre was added to the Gerald Larkin Academic Building across the street.

25. Munk Centre for International Studies
Eden Smith & Sons, 1909
Renovation and additions *Kuwabara Payne McKenna Blumberg Architects, 2000*
David Bosanquet Gardens *Martin Lane Fox, 2000*

Named after Canadian businessman Peter Munk, this hub for interdisciplinary academic research on global issues is located on the Trinity College campus and houses more than forty centers and programs, along with Trinity's John W. Graham Library. The pleasing U-shaped building focuses on the formal David Bosanquet Gardens, designed by the well-known English landscape gardener Martin Lane Fox and among the university's most elegant outdoor rooms.

The three buildings that are now linked to form the Munk Centre were originally built in 1909 as separate residence halls for men and were then considered state-of-the-art. That year's August issue of the magazine *Construction* noted that the red New Brunswick stone and red pressed brick dormitories were most successfully planned, and all three are similar in design, construction and arrangement. They are composed around a quadrangle which has a roadway forming the line of demarcation on its open side. The general architectural effect is derived from straight, broad lines, perfect proportions, simple surfaces and a well balanced door and window arrangement.

In fact, the architect of these long, slender buildings, Eden Smith, became well-known in Toronto for designing progressive housing with a strong sense of community, exemplified by his Spruce Court (1913) and Riverdale Courts (1914) projects for the Toronto Housing Company. These provided affordable accommodations for working-class people and signaled an important beginning for the involvement of both Toronto and Ontario in publicly supported housing.

In 2000 Kuwabara Payne McKenna Blumberg Architects knit together the three former residence halls with an enclosed arcade (similar to the one at Woodsworth College, discussed on page 122). They extended two east-west wings westward toward Devonshire Place, creating light-filled meeting rooms faced in pink-gray granite on the exterior. Slender steel finials provide a subtle vertical thrust at these end rooms and reference the ornament of Massey College across the street.

26. Massey College
Thompson, Berwick & Pratt (Ron Thom, project architect), 1963
Renovations *Shim-Sutcliffe Architects, 1998, 2001, 2002, 2005*

If there is a "most loved" modern building on the St. George campus, it is surely Massey College, located at the northwest corner of Hoskin Avenue and Devonshire Place. On the surface, the explanation for the accolades is simple: the image Massey presents is architecturally unthreatening, and its textures, intimate spaces, and ornamentation generate feelings of warmth and security. But the story of this small institution and its success is considerably more complex.

Massey College, a gift of the Massey family and the Massey Foundation, is an interdisciplinary residential college with a community consisting of 130 junior fellows (60 resident, 70 nonresident), senior fellows, senior residents, and the master (the chief administrative officer). Plans to create Massey College were considered as early as 1957 but not fully formalized until 1960, when Vincent Massey organized a national design competition. The committee for the competition included Vincent Massey's son, Hart, and his nephew Geoffrey, both of whom were architects and supporters of modernism.

Ron Thom, then a partner in the Vancouver-based firm Thompson, Berwick & Pratt, and not well-known beyond the West Coast, submitted the winning design,

ABOVE: *Massey College*

BOTTOM: *Massey College, Ondaatje Hall*

which included a total of five residences, each with their own internal staircase, in the east, west, and north wings of a quadrangle building on the constricted site (150 by 300 feet), and clustered the master's lodge, library, common room, and dining rooms at the south end, along with a gatehouse. The chapel and a round room for meetings of the College Corporation were located at the northwest corner. The architect anchored the composition with a tall clock tower at the south end of the quadrangle, near the main entrance.

Prince Philip, Duke of Edinburgh, laid the cornerstone on May 25, 1962, and the building opened in 1963 to both fanfare and controversy. For many modernists, it was too traditional, and for many traditionalists, it was too modern. Indeed, Thom's very personal creative approach avoided stylistic labels and fused modernist and traditional sensibilities. On the one hand, he designed a quadrangle-type building as the competition committee had requested, inspired by the colleges of Oxford and Cambridge; on the other hand, he created highly abstract, shifting planes (as seen in the college's perimeter walls along the street edges and in the clock tower), recalling the work of the Dutch modernist W. M. Dudok as well as the Dutch de Stijl movement of the early twentieth century. Permeating the whole design were strong influences from the American architect Frank Lloyd Wright, whose principles for an organic architecture had inspired Thom, filtered through his own experience of the naturalism of British Columbia. Furthermore, Thom had the audacity to add ornament to Massey College's design at a time when the minimalist International Style, which promoted a sleek, industrial look, was most popular. In retrospect, it is not surprising that Thom, sometimes affectionately called "Frank Lloyd Thom," struck nerves in Toronto, where he moved in 1963 and set up his own practice, eventually delivering major projects such as the remarkable Trent University in nearby Peterborough, Ontario.

The story of Massey College would be incomplete without mentioning some of its superb interior spaces. The Junior Common Room, located at the building's south end, is simultaneously compressive (it has a relatively low ceiling) and expansive (stepping down in section to large windows that face the quadrangle on one side and a narrow, walled courtyard on the other). The space exudes warmth. Located directly above is the main dining hall, Ondaatje Hall, a mysterious, lantern-like room. It hovers slightly above the rest of the college, gently announcing its importance. Here, Thom masterfully and magically manipulated natural light, making the hall one of the greatest rooms in the university. Nearby is a diminutive private dining room, where the College Charter is exhibited along with the Nobel Gold Medal for Chemistry, presented to the college by Professor John Polanyi, recipient of the medal in 1986 and one of the founding fellows of the college. In recent years, a series of thoughtful, almost seamless renovations have been completed by Shim-Sutcliffe Architects.

27. Newman Centre of Toronto

Attributed to David Roberts, 1890

Ballroom addition *George M. Miller, 1901*

St. Thomas Aquinas Church *Arthur W. Holmes, 1927*

Newman Centre of Toronto

Among the grand homes that lined St. George Street in the nineteenth and early twentieth centuries, number 89, which is now the Newman Centre of Toronto, was one of the most spectacular. It was built in 1890 for Wilmot D. Matthews, whose family fortune came from the grain trading business. A hybrid of the Richardsonian Romanesque and Queen Anne-revival styles, the red brick house is anchored at its southwest corner by a three-story cylindrical volume, echoed at the rear of the house by a second, somewhat smaller cylinder topped by a covered porch. In addition to red brick, the house's materials palette also includes Credit Valley sandstone walls, a slate roof, and unglazed terra-cotta decorative elements. The building's many gables have elaborately carved vergeboards and scalloped wood shingles.

The Newman Centre of Toronto (formerly the Newman Foundation), which operates under the umbrella of the Archdiocese of Toronto and fosters dialogue between the Roman Catholic Church and the modern world, purchased the Matthews house in 1922. Admirably, the house has since been treated well, including the interior, which contains some of the finest late-nineteenth-century rooms in Toronto, featuring wood-paneled walls, basket-weave oak floors with edge banding, coffered ceilings, plaster moldings, stained glass, and elaborate hardware. The vaulted ballroom added to the building's south end in 1901, for the wedding of the Matthews' eldest daughter, is outstanding, including its highly sculptural brick chimney.

Soon after it bought the house, the Newman Foundation tore down a coach house at the rear of the property and in 1926/27 constructed St. Thomas Aquinas Church, which is designed in the style of fifteenth-century Gothic architecture, with exterior walls of broken-face Credit Valley limestone and ashlar Indiana limestone, and a roof of gray slate and copper. Inside, we find arch-braced trusses and an exposed ceiling of dark-stained British Columbia fir.

Joseph L. Rotman School of Management

28. Joseph L. Rotman School of Management
Zeidler Partnership Architects, 1995; **addition,** *2006*
South addition *Kuwabara Payne McKenna Blumberg Architects, 2011*

Named in honor of Joseph L. Rotman, past chairman, CEO, and founder of Clairvest Group, Inc., and known simply as "Rotman," the university's business school is housed in a distinctive, if difficult to categorize, building. Some of its architectural aspects are fairly normal and polite, such as the lower red-brick portion, which relates comfortably to the historic houses along St. George Street and the Innis College Student Residence next door (also designed by Eberhard Zeidler). This sense of the familiar is short-lived, though, because parts of the building seem to have broken loose—bending inward, folding outward, jagging upward—making it look like an agitated mouse-gray iceberg. Shardlike zinc and glass forms protrude as elongated dormers and sculptural skylights. One of Rotman's most memorable spaces is the faculty and staff lounge, which juts from the third floor at the northwest corner and reads as an amalgam of Victorian, modernist, and deconstructivist sensibilities. Most interior spaces are less fanciful than this, though, including the three-story central atrium, an attractive rectangular multipurpose hall around which the school is organized.

Rotman recently commenced an ambitious addition to the south, designed by Kuwabara Payne McKenna Blumberg Architects, which will provide space for the Desautels Centre for Integrative Thinking, the Lloyd and Delphine Martin Prosperity Institute, and other divisions, allowing the Rotman School to double its enrollment by 2014. The project will incorporate the historic John Downey House at 97 St. George Street, which contains a marvelous chapel on the second floor designed for the Canadian Missionary Society by Sproatt & Rolph and completed in 1930. Extending south toward the Newman Centre and west to the existing pedestrian lane, the Rotman addition will finally give identity to a parcel of the campus that has been ill-defined for several decades.

29. Innis College Student Residence

Zeidler Partnership Architects, 1994

Innis College Student Residence

Serving Innis College, located directly across St. George Street, the U-shaped student residence has over eighty apartment-style bedroom units. Within the "U" is an informal courtyard, contained at the open end by a semicircular fountain. The main entrance to the six-story building is marked by a large steel arch with an abstracted keystone (also made of steel), above which are stacked bay windows with steel articulations. The volumetric and material complexity displayed here is representative of that found throughout the building. Architect Eberhard Zeidler wanted the residence

Woodsworth College courtyard

to relate in scale, texture, and color to the numerous Victorian and Edwardian houses along St. George Street, and in this sense the project is successful. A year later, Zeidler completed the Joseph L. Rotman School of Management directly to the south, and the two buildings share a pleasant forecourt with a family of exuberant glass canopies.

30. Woodsworth College
Kuwabara Payne McKenna Blumberg Architects in association with Barton Myers Associates, Inc., 1992
119 St. George (Alexander McArthur House) *David B. Dick, 1892*
Alterations *Francis S. Baker, 1911*
Kruger Hall *Allward & Gouinlock Architects, 1947*

Established in 1974 with a focus on part-time students in the Faculty of Arts and Science, Woodsworth College has more than 6,300 students, of which a majority are now full-time, coming directly from high school. The college was named for J. S. Woodsworth, an advocate for social justice and founder of the Canadian political party the Co-operative Commonwealth Federation (CCF), forerunner of the New Democratic Party (NDP).

Tucked discreetly behind three renovated mansions on St. George Street and organized around a long, narrow courtyard, Woodsworth College—designed by Barton Myers—is one of the university's most thoughtfully and rigorously crafted projects of the past two decades. The new wings, arranged in an L-shape, march along in a rational, disciplined manner, faced in custom-made, pinkish-orange brick rising from a base of gray granite. Myers used extensive wood detailing along with elegant steel elements to architecturally articulate and differentiate. The complex has numerous entrances, and the principal one at the south is marked by a distinctive tower sheathed in thin panels of pink onyx. Woodsworth College is reminiscent of the work of Louis Kahn—modern, but embedded in the classical tradition. This could be because Myers studied under Kahn at the University of Pennsylvania and worked with him following graduation.

As an infill, adaptive-reuse project, Woodsworth imaginatively incorporates the 1892 Alexander McArthur House and the 1941 officers' quarters for the Canadian Officer Training Corp. that had been erected alongside the house. Now accommodating the college's administrative offices and various student functions, these buildings are the heart of Woodsworth. The renovated spaces flow gracefully into a delightful sky-lit cafe, which is anchored at the south end by a monumental fireplace. The 1888 John R. Bailey house at 121 St. George Street (now the Centre for Industrial and Human Resources) appears to be part of Woodsworth (and contributes walls and terraces along the west side) but is actually a separate division of the university.

One could argue that the second heart of the college is the Peter F. Bronfman Courtyard, an inviting gathering place surrounded by a gracious indoor-outdoor, cloisterlike corridor. At the courtyard's northeast corner the architects included a distinctive octagonal boardroom. Following a long run of mediocre architecture in the 1970s and 1980s, the university took note of the exceptional Woodsworth project, which was guided by the college's vice principal and registrar, Dr. Alex R. Waugh. Woodsworth became a symbol of quality and a rallying point for both progressive architecture and the implementation of a new process for selecting architects. Consequently, in 1997 the university's Design Review Committee was established, which continues to advise on architectural design matters on the three campuses.

31. Department and Centre for the Study of Religion
Burke and Horwood, 1900

The noted Toronto architect Edmund Burke designed this fantastic house, which was the home of Thomas M. Harris, a partner in Smith Brothers, a large carriage and wagon manufacturer, and his wife. The house now serves the Department and Centre for the Study of Religion. Noteworthy architectural features include the scalloped wood shingles on the front gable and the deeply recessed, arched entry, which is surrounded with beautifully carved red sandstone. Burke was also the author of the Architecture Building (see page 140).

Woodsworth College Residence

32. Woodsworth College Residence
Architects Alliance, 2004

The northern gateway of the University of Toronto's St. George campus is accentuated by the twenty-one-story Woodsworth College Residence, which provides accommodation for almost four hundred students in apartmentlike suites. The building's composition consists of a U-shaped, four-story podium from which a seventeen-story glass tower rises. The outdoor space formed by the podium, the Alex R. Waugh Courtyard, opens to the south and connects to the main Woodsworth College building, linking to an attractive new east-west walkway lined with a double row of birch trees.

The podium is transparent at its base and more solid from the second to fourth levels, where it is clad in yellow brick, divided into panels by vertical window slots that establish an irregular and not entirely pleasing rhythm. The tower, wrapped in glass panels varying in shade and color, is more architecturally successful than the podium. Some of the tower's faces are rendered in a cheeky checkerboard pattern that recalls the populist side of mid-twentieth-century modernism, along with the work of the trailblazing Toronto modernist, architect Peter Dickinson.

Admissions and Awards Building

33. Admissions and Awards Building *Burke and Horwood, 1909*

A small brass plaque on the iron fence in front of the Admissions and Awards Building reads simply "Meteorological Office." Nearby, a larger plaque explains the story behind this mysterious title, which began when the British Army conducted meteorological and magnetic observations at the university in 1840. In 1853 Canada took over the program and built a new observatory, which became the headquarters of the Meteorological Service of Canada, providing a system of stations that by 1876 enabled the service to issue storm forecasts and warnings. In 1909 the Meteorological Service built its new headquarters (the Dominion Meteorological Building), designed by Burke and Horwood, at 315 Bloor Street West—a function the building served until 1971, when the university purchased it for use as its Admissions and Awards Building.

The structure's heavily rusticated Miramichi sandstone facade gives it a rugged, fortresslike feel. Its symmetrical composition is offset by a cylindrical, medieval-looking tower at the southeast corner, which originally had a domed observatory housing a telescope. Also of note are the elegant windows on the top floor, which have delicately articulated mullions. A tiny structure—rotated slightly to be oriented due north—is located at the west side of the building. Likely constructed at the same time as the Meteorological Office, its original purpose is a matter of broad conjecture.

34. Ontario Institute for Studies in Education (OISE)
Kenneth R. Cooper, 1968

Established by the province of Ontario in 1965 as a center for graduate studies and research in education, the Ontario Institute for Studies in Education, or "OISE," symbolized the progressive 1960s institutionally and architecturally in Canada. Completed one year after Expo '67 in Montreal, the OISE building displays the optimism of that bold venture. The institute, which became affiliated with the university

LEFT: *Ontario Institute for Studies in Education*
RIGHT: *Factor-Inwentash Faculty of Social Work*

in 1966 and fully integrated in 1996, serves some 1,800 graduate students, 1,300 students training to be teachers, and more than 6,500 students taking continuing education classes.

OISE's narrow frontage on Bloor Street West disguises the immensity of this poured-in-place and prefabricated concrete building, which is best viewed from the east on Bedford Road or from the parking lot of the York Club to the west. From these vantage points, one can fully appreciate the two huge tower wings with their faceted, light-manipulating facades. A long, well-proportioned colonnade runs along the west side of the building, leading to the main entrance, the education commons, a five hundred-seat auditorium, and an entrance to the subway. Brick, natural wood, and quarry tile warm OISE's interior, which displays modern art by Jack Bush, Sorel Etrog, and Kazuo Nakamura.

Although not exactly loved when it was completed in 1968, the OISE building has recently gathered a new following among young architects.

35. Factor-Inwentash Faculty of Social Work
Marani & Morris, 1950
renovations *Dubois Plumb Partnership, 1999*

This building at the northwest corner of Bloor Street West and Bedford Road epitomizes the conservative approach architects Marani & Morris held onto at a time when many Toronto firms fully embraced the wave of post–World War II mod-

Varsity Stadium

ernism that swept across North America. Completed in 1950 as an office building for Texaco, the structure is interesting in relation to Marani & Morris's design for the Bank of Canada on University Avenue of 1958. Both are classically composed (bilaterally symmetrical with an expression of base, middle, and top) and severely rational. However, the former lacks the deluxe materials and refinement of detail found in the Bank of Canada building. The School of Social Work (now the Factor-Inwentash Faculty of Social Work, named in recognition of philanthropists Lynn Factor and Sheldon Inwentash) moved into the former Texaco building in 1970. Dubois Plumb Partnership completed a series of handsome interior renovations in 1999.

36. Varsity Centre

Stadium *Harkness Loudon & Hertzberg (engineers), 1924*
Stadium master plan *Craig Madill and Loudon, 1929*
Arena *Darling & Pearson with Harkness Loudon & Hertzberg as engineers, 1926*
Stadium addition and renovations *Proctor, Redfern & Laughlin (engineers), 1950*
New stadium *Diamond + Schmitt Architects in association with Ellerbe Becket Architects, 2006*

The University of Toronto's Varsity Centre includes a five-thousand-seat stadium, a four-hundred-meter eight-lane track, an artificial-turf field (with an air-supported

LEFT: *Varsity Centre arcade*
RIGHT: *Edward Johnson Building*

polyester dome for winter use), and a four-thousand-seat hockey arena. This sports and recreation facility welcomes and encourages all levels of physical activity, from the high performance of competitive athletes to everyday casual exercise.

The site's history is worth recounting. Before 1898 the university's football team, the "Blues," played in King's College Circle. When the sometimes rowdy games drew complaints, the Blues moved to a site at the location of today's Varsity Centre. In 1901 the first cinder track was created, along with a grandstand seating five hundred people; and in 1911 the university constructed Varsity Stadium. Built primarily of wood, it had a capacity of 7,200, soon increased to 10,500. A reinforced concrete grandstand was constructed in 1924, raising the center's capacity to 16,000 people, and two years later the 4,000-seat Varsity Arena was added to the east.

In the late 1920s, James H. Craig and Henry Harrison Madill, in collaboration with engineering professor Thomas R. Loudon, designed a new horseshoe-shaped stadium, which was going to make Varsity Centre the largest football stadium in Canada. But World War Two delayed the project, and the major renovation was not completed until 1950, with a capacity of 21,767 rather than the hoped for 35,000.

By the mid-1990s Varsity Stadium had become run down, but the land it sat on, particularly along Bloor Street West, was quite valuable. The university considered several grandiose scenarios including major commercial development along Bloor Street West, with a new stadium to the south. It was soon realized, though, that the site was too tight for this grand vision. A subsequent imaginative, comprehensive plan for the Bloor Street/Devonshire Place that included a new stadium, student housing, and modest commercial development also proved unworkable, as did a 2004 plan for a one hundred million dollar complex that included a football stadium for the Toronto Argonauts.

The old stadium was finally demolished in 2002, and in 2006 the decade of debate over what to do with its site ended with the opening of the modest Varsity Centre, which features a five-thousand-seat stadium with west-facing seating above a covered arcade that leads to the 1926 Varsity Arena.

37. Edward Johnson Building
Gordon Adamson & Associates, 1961
Addition *Moffat Kinoshita Associates Inc., 1987*

Set on a concrete plinth that rises from the bottom of the Philosopher's Walk valley, the Faculty of Music's Edward Johnson Building has a formal air about it, graced by twenty-four slender concrete columns around its perimeter. From the east, the three primary parts of the building, which was named for Edward Johnson, who was general manager of the Metropolitan Opera in New York and a member of the university board of governors, are evident: the main two-story concrete and glass volume, the brick-clad library hovering over the main part, and the brick stagehouse rising at the north. The main entrance is situated off center within the eight-bay east facade and leads to a grand lobby with a pair of monumental lightwells that pierce the ceiling and a third-floor lounge. These wells are capped by delirious skylights that look like enormous flowers whose eight "petals" are circular glazed units. From the lobby one enters the 815-seat MacMillan Theatre, designed for orchestral concerts and operas. On the lower floor, level with Philosopher's Walk, is the 490-seat Walter Hall, created for chamber music and recitals, and one of Toronto's finest small auditoriums.

Although the Edward Johnson Building works well architecturally, its relationship to nearby buildings and streets is poor, as it is sandwiched awkwardly between Falconer Hall, McLaughlin Planetarium, the Royal Ontario Museum, and Philosopher's Walk. Unfortunately, its attractive front looks directly into the rear of Falconer Hall. With new plans afoot for this precinct, including the transformation of the Faculty of Law and the addition of a major project on the planetarium site by the Royal Ontario Museum, the Edward Johnson Building will soon be recontextualized and finally given a proper setting.

38. Faculty of Law (Flavelle House) *Darling & Pearson, 1902*
Library addition *Hart Massey and William J. McBain, 1961*
Renovations and additions *Moffat Kinoshita Associates, 1989*
Renovations to Flavelle House *Taylor Hariri Pontarini, 2001*
Master plan for renewal *Hariri Pontarini, 2008*

The heart of the Faculty of Law is an imposing mansion at the northwest corner of Queen's Park. Best described as Edwardian-Georgian in style, it was built for Sir Joseph Wesley Flavelle, who expanded his meatpacking business into Canada's first nationwide retail grocery chain.

The University of Toronto set up the residential neighborhood around Queen's Park in 1861, and homes for the wealthy appeared soon afterward. Flavelle chose

Faculty of Law (Flavelle House)

Darling & Pearson–who were also the architects of the Canadian Bank of Commerce where Flavelle had been a director–to design his new home, Holwood, which was to have both the comfort and the charm of country homes he had admired in the south of England. The mansion consists of a main two-story wing and a three-story service wing set at an angle. A pedimented pavilion containing the main stair negotiates this obtuse angle. Darling & Pearson gave Holwood a grand portico supported by Corinthian columns finished in stucco, into which they set an elegantly framed door with slender Ionic colonnettes. (A duplicate portico faces west at the rear of the house.)

Within, Holwood's fine rooms have been preserved. To the right of the entrance, the former music room focuses on an elegant fireplace graced by a Jacobean oak mantle. The magnificent barrel-vaulted ceiling was decorated with art nouveau angels by Gustav Hahn. Flavelle died in 1939, leaving his home to the University of Toronto.

Although the principal north-facing facade has been preserved, numerous additions and renovations have dramatically changed the setting of the mansion over the years. In 1961 an overtly modern structure designed by architects Hart Massey and William J. McBain was added on the sloping, wooded area to the south, housing a new law library and lecture rooms. The architects' idea was to keep the original mansion and new buildings separate and distinct, which they achieved by creating a delicate, transparent glass link between the two. It was an extremely thoughtful solution but, alas, the 1961 wing was later consumed by a bombastic, unsympathetic transformation in 1989–a structure that is particularly unsightly when seen from Philosopher's Walk. The Faculty of Law now requires more space and is looking forward to a comprehensive architectural renewal, which will provide an opportunity to resituate and once again celebrate the marvelous Flavelle House.

39. Falconer Hall *Sproatt & Rolph, 1902*

For the small building it is, Edwardian-style Falconer Hall, which houses part of the Faculty of Law, has had a complex history. Its multiple lives started in 1902 as Wymilwood, the home of the financier Edward R. Wood, vice president and managing director of Central Canada Loan & Savings, and his wife, Agnes. The Woods donated the house to Victoria University in 1925 as a women's residence.

Falconer Hall

In 1949 ownership was transferred to the University of Toronto, and in 1952 the building was renamed "Falconer Hall" to honor the university's fourth president, Robert Falconer, as part of a plan to build a new women's athletic center on the site. Architects Fleury & Arthur drafted a plan for the athletic center, which was to preserve and reuse Falconer Hall as a women's social and meeting center. Early in 1955, the Woods' former coach house and servants' quarters were demolished to make way for the new building. However, the provincial government subsequently stopped the project, which it considered too large and too close to the Legislative Building. A new site for the athletic center was found west of St. George Street, where the Women's Athletic Building was completed in 1959 (now called the Clara Benson Building).

From 1959 to 1961, Falconer Hall was briefly the home of the fledgling York University, before the Faculty of Law took over the building. It will soon be reborn as part of the renewal of the area that includes the Flavelle House, the Edward Johnson Building, and the McLaughlin Planetarium.

WALK FOUR: THE SOUTHWEST CAMPUS

SPADINA CRESCENT

HOSKIN AVENUE

BACK CAMPUS

HARBORD STREET

SPADINA AVENUE

WILLCOCKS STREET

HURON STREET

57

56

55

54

53

52

52

51

50

58

59

RUSSELL STREET

48

49

ST. GEORGE STREET

42

47

46

43

44

41

40

COLLEGE STREET

45

Walk Four: The Southwest Campus

Up until the early 1950s, the university's central St. George campus extended north-south from Bloor Street to College Street and east-west from Queen's Park to St. George Street. With mounting enrollment pressures after World War Two, plans emerged to expand the campus west of St. George Street to Spadina Avenue. Although a planning committee report from 1949 supported this proposition, it was not until 1956 that a west campus designation was finally approved, identifying a thirty-three-acre area bounded by St. George Street, College Street, Spadina Avenue, and Harbord Street. In the meantime, however, two new university structures were built "beyond the border"—the Central Steam Plant (1952) and the School of Nursing (1953)—signaling that the westward movement had already begun.

The Plateau Committee, an advisory planning committee set up by the university's board of governors, envisioned that the new western precinct would be devoid of automobiles, full of green spaces, and designed for pedestrians. A January 1960 article on University of Toronto campus development in *The Journal of the Royal Architectural Institute of Canada* emphatically stated that "the exclusion of automobiles from campus areas is of prime importance," and it was also asserted that "all buildings on the West Campus would be simple and economical in construction and maintenance." The university imagined underground service access, and pedestrian overpasses and underpasses to allow students to move easily and safely across St. George Street from the old campus to the new, airy western side. There would be two large athletic fields and parking structures along Spadina Avenue to buffer the nascent Spadina Expressway. This grand vision, however, was laid to rest in 1957 due to funding problems, resulting in the patchwork planning of the past half-century.

Nevertheless, campus master plans from the 1960s through the early 1990s slowly edged toward an emphasis on pedestrians, with one plan even calling for the complete removal of vehicles from St. George Street in order to unify the east and west areas as a "walking campus." The construction of the Earth Sciences Centre in 1989, which included the pedestrianization of Bancroft Avenue, and the completion of the 1979 Warren Stevens Building, which transformed Classic Avenue into a benign service lane, went some distance toward realizing the dream of a landscaped and pedestrian-friendly west campus. It was not until 1996, though, when St. George Street itself was completely transformed under the leadership of planner and philanthropist Judy Matthews, that the university community started talking seriously again about the necessity for high-quality, pedestrian-friendly open space on campus.

With Matthews's prodding, in 1999 the university initiated a comprehensive open-space master plan, called "Investing in the Landscape," drafted by the

Wilson Gate, St. George Street

landscape architecture firms Urban Strategies, Inc. and Corban and Goode Landscape Architecture and Urbanism, along with Taylor Hariri Pontarini Architects. The plan's guiding principles have allowed the incremental reknitting of the southwest campus's fragmented landscape.

40. St. George Street, Wilson Gate, and Perly Rae Gate
Brown + Storey Architects and van Nostrand DiCastri Architects, with Corban and Goode Landscape Architecture and Urbanism, 1996

St. George Street, the busy public thoroughfare that runs north-south through the campus, had been problematic since World War Two. Widened in 1948 to accommodate more traffic at higher speeds, it was not only hazardous for students crossing from the old campus to the west campus, it was also unsightly. In the mid-1990s, the university, the city of Toronto, and urban activist-planner Judy Matthews set out to correct the situation by narrowing and calming the street; substantially widening sidewalks; and adding imaginative retaining walls, curbs, benches, planters, and bicycle racks, along with hundreds of trees.

This substantial undertaking had strong conceptual underpinnings. The project's architects and landscape architects devised a family of thick, angular concrete elements that are multivalent: they retain soil, protect trees, define circulation paths, and provide places to sit. At either end of the five-block-long area, these energetic concrete forms bend and increase in scale, and are topped by conical steel "gateposts" to mark entrances to the campus. The south entry, called the Wilson Gate, honors Ann Elizabeth Wilson, who, along with her husband, former University of Toronto President Robert J. Prichard, was a strong supporter of the St. George Street revitalization. Similarly designed, the north Perly Rae Gate honors Arlene Perly Rae, journalist, arts patron, and wife of Bob Rae, who was premier of Ontario from 1990 to 1995.

As a result, the street has not only been transformed into a pedestrian-friendly corridor, it has also become a *place*—an elongated plaza of sorts—that finally binds the historic central campus to the west campus. In the past decade, thoughtfully landscaped tentacles have branched out east and west from St. George—including the Sir Daniel Wilson, Nona Macdonald, and Woodsworth College walkways and the Davenport Chemical Research Building/Lash Miller Chemical Laboratories Garden—generating further spatial connectivity and social interaction.

41. Koffler Student Services Centre

Alfred H. Chapman in association with Wickson & Gregg, 1908
Addition *Chapman & Oxley in association with Wickson & Gregg, 1930*
Theater renovation *Irving Grossman, 1961*
Renovation and restoration *Howard D. Chapman and Howard V. Walker, 1985*

In 1905 the city of Toronto announced a national design competition for a new central reference library that was also to incorporate a College Street branch library. Alfred H. Chapman's winning beaux arts design features a grand entrance at the building's east end that rises up to the reference library on the *piano nobile*, balanced by a lesser entrance at the west end to the ground-floor branch library. The reference and reading room overlooked College Street through two-story windows set between Corinthian pilasters. The processional entry sequence, moving up and through the marble-lined entrance hall and, finally, to the third floor, is memorable. In 1930 Chapman & Oxley completed a handsome addition along St. George Street.

The stately building was taken over by the university in the early 1980s and converted into the Koffler Student Services Centre, which also houses the university bookstore. Fortunately, the building's primary spaces were preserved and restored, although the bookstore functions have always seemed shoehorned into the historic spaces. A three-story postmodern concourse with seven Pop-scale mustard-colored arches, completed in 1985, was not a positive addition and lacks the subtlety of the original building. In 2002 the center's north elevation was restored and carefully incorporated into the atrium of the new Bahen Centre for Information Technology.

Koffler Student Services Center

42. Bahen Centre for Information Technology
Diamond + Schmitt Architects, 2002

The Bahen Centre for Information Technology, part of the Faculty of Applied Science and Engineering (FASE), is conveniently located opposite the engineering buildings on St. George Street. The center's multidisciplinary program, which includes the Faculty of Arts and Science as an integral partner, supports facilities for teaching and research in computer science, electrical engineering, engineering science, mechanical engineering, and industrial engineering.

Although its front door is on St. George Street, the L-shaped, cream-color brick building extends deep into the block and can be entered from the north, east, south, and west. It is attached to the Koffler Student Services Centre, abuts the Central Steam Plant, and incorporates and reuses a historic Victorian house. It also embraces the Fields Institute for Research in Mathematical Sciences to the west. The entire complex sits on top of an underground parking garage and implements a "green" agenda that extends from the building's systems to its underlying urban infill and densification strategies. A wonderful "urban octopus," the center reaches out and pulls spaces, activities, and people together, reinforcing its multidisciplinary agenda.

The Bahen Centre's sprawling composition is held together by a monumental atrium that runs east-west through the entire building. Soaring, polished concrete columns articulate this beautiful space, which is flooded with natural light from above. At the atrium's west end, a cylindrical volume incorporating stairs and lounges rises dramatically through eight levels and marks the minor cross-axis running north-south.

A sculpturally ambitious convex volume pushes out at the building's south side and terminates a narrow visual corridor and gently rising pedestrian route from College Street. At the base of this volume is a granite-paved courtyard defined by the Bahen Centre, the Koffler Centre, the Fields Institute, and the Architecture Building. A series of cylindrical columnlike towers (which store rainwater for irrigation) give further definition to the western edge of the courtyard, which is an attractive place with cascading pools flowing down to College Street, and a cafe at its northern edge.

43. Fields Institute for Research in Mathematical Sciences *Kuwabara Payne McKenna Blumberg Architects, 1995*

Founded in 1991 as an advanced institute for research in mathematical sciences, the Fields Institute, known as "The Fields," is named in honor of John Charles Fields, professor of mathematics at the University of Toronto, who became well known for establishing the Fields Medal, often called the "Nobel Prize in Mathematics."

The institute is set back from College Street to align with the Koffler Student Services Centre to the east, and the two buildings share a long, landscaped zone terminated by the Architecture Building to the west. Clad in rusticated limestone and red brick, The Fields's public face projects decorum and good urban manners. Note the subtle game of chamfered corners at the southeast and southwest, which turn toward nearby buildings and create special corner rooms.

The exterior politeness continues inside, but with a few twists. On the second level, a helical stair and a wood-burning fireplace animate a three-story atrium,

Bahen Centre for Information Technology

which incorporates the James Stewart Library at the north. A Douglas-fir ceiling plane hovers overhead, with natural light streaming in around the edges of this warm, communal space. At the rear, the communal area spills onto a terrace overlooking the Bahen Centre courtyard.

44. Architecture Building (John H. Daniels Faculty of Architecture, Landscape, and Design)

Burke, Horwood & White, 1909
North addition *Molesworth, West and Secord, 1920*
Addition *Kohn Shnier Architects, 2000*

If you look carefully above the front door of the Architecture Building, you will notice a horizontal stone plaque with very faint traces of the inscription "Royal College of Dental Surgeons," revealing the structure's first use. The five-story brick building served dentistry students from 1909 until 1958; in 1961 the architecture department took it over. Now the building houses the John H. Daniels Faculty of Architecture, Landscape, and Design.

Designed by the influential Toronto architect Edmund Burke, who was the principal author of the downtown Robert Simpson Company department store and the Bloor Street Viaduct, the Architecture Building is essentially a turn-of-the-century Chicago-inspired "industrial" structure with an overlay of prairie-style motifs. The tripartite facades include a banded brick base, a middle section containing the main floor and mezzanine, and a more elaborate top section composed of loftlike spaces, formerly the dental school's laboratories and clinics and now "design lab" studios. Originally, a simple classical cornice (now hidden) completed the composition. Four-story brick pilasters articulate the corners of the building, while engaged pilasters enliven the two upper stories. The top floor has small brick piers, topped with prairie-style capitals. A handsomely sculpted portal frames the main entrance.

In 1997 a master plan was established for incrementally adding to and renovating the Architecture Building to accommodate the school's expanding graduate programs. The first addition, completed in 2000, was a sleek, cantilevered "bay window" by Kohn Shnier Architects at the building's southeast corner, bringing extra space and natural light to the school's Shore + Moffat Library and Eric Arthur Gallery. A series of spirited interior renovations has been completed over the past decade. The school is named in honor of John H. Daniels, a graduate of the school of architecture and highly successful developer, who made a major donation to the faculty in 2008.

45. Gage Building *Charles S. Cobb, 1914*

Gage Building

This solid little building was built for the National Sanitarium Association and was in honor of Sir William J. Gage, best known for advancing the diagnosis and treatment of tuberculosis. Located at the corner of College and Ross streets, the building faces both east and north. Employing the Georgian-revival style, the architect, Charles S. Cobb, astutely addressed the particular urban corner condition, creating similar elevations on the east and north but with subtle differentiation. Miraculously, period detailing such as external handrails and finely crafted door hardware has survived.

The Gage Building, with its fundamental architectural integrity, is a pleasant surprise. The legacy of Cobb, who designed several significant Toronto buildings, deserves broader recognition. Among his best works was the grand beaux arts City Registry Office on Albert Street (1917), demolished in 1960 to make way for Toronto's new City Hall.

46. Centre for Addiction and Mental Health (CAMH)

250 College Street *John B. Parkin Associates, 1966*
33 Russell Street *Marani, Rounthwaite & Dick, 1969*

Centre for Addiction and Mental Health

Within the complex that makes up the province of Ontario's Centre for Addiction and Mental Health (CAMH), the most imposing building is the precast concrete-clad tower (and attached low block to the north) at 250 College Street. These started life in 1966 as the province's Clarke Institute of Psychiatry, the main teaching hospital for psychiatry at the University of Toronto. At the end of the 1960s two buildings were constructed to house the Addiction Research Foundation at 33 Russell Street, completing the campus. In 1998 the Clarke Institute of Psychiatry, the Addiction Research Foundation, the Queen Street Mental Health Centre, and the Donwood Institute merged to form a new public entity, the Centre for Addiction and Mental Health, with which the university remains affiliated. (At the time of writing this book, the minicampus was undergoing an occupancy transition, and the CAMH had started moving to new quarters on Queen Street West.)

Among mid-twentieth-century corporate architectural practices in Toronto, the firm of John B. Parkin Associates looms large, having attained a status akin to that of Skidmore, Owings & Merrill (SOM) in the United States. The commission to design the Clarke, as the institute is known, came only a few years after the firm designed the university's Sidney Smith Hall. If one ignores the Clarke's entrance pavilion (a later addition) and the unsightly wing to the west, picturing the tower as a clean, ground-up extrusion of concrete, it remains an authoritative work of architecture. The scale of the three-story base, with its jazzlike rhythm of alternating elongated windows and concrete panels (the latter looking like disguised columns) is convincing. The disciplined wrapping of the tower's main body with precast concrete units and the slightly protruding concrete screen at its top that hides mechanical equipment add to the building's visual appeal.

215 Huron Street

The buildings at 33 Russell Street are another story. Here we find a low concrete block linked to a squat brick tower, forming a mazelike territory of landscaped
roofs, plazas, and service entries. The low building vaguely recalls Kallmann,
McKinnell and Knowles's 1969 Boston City Hall (which in turn is indebted to Le
Corbusier's 1960 La Tourette Dominican monastery near Lyon), and its overriding
concrete frame is mildly interesting. But on the whole, the 33 Russell Street buildings are architecturally awkward and do little to reinforce Spadina Crescent, the
important urban space that they join at the northwest.

47. 215 Huron Street   *Chapman & Hurst, 1959*

In the late 1950s and early 1960s, the university was expanding rapidly and
urgently needed a central servicing facility that included workshop and maintenance areas, storage, and physical plant administrative offices. Originally called the
"Superintendent's Building," it consisted of a ground floor with two levels of offices
above. The unassuming, utilitarian structure was an early example of a "fast track"
project, designed in a highly rationalized manner that allowed the ground floor maintenance and workshop area to be completed in four-and-a-half months and put into
operation while the two office floors, clad simply in precast concrete panels with
long bands of continuous windows, were finished above. Additional office floors

were added a few years later. Near the main entrance is a decorative concrete panel designed by Dora de Pedery-Hunt. The building currently houses numerous divisions, including the Department of Philosophy.

48. Anthropology Building *Basil G. Ludlow & Partners, 1963*

Anthropology Building

Formerly the F. Norman Hughes Pharmacy Building, this modest brick-clad cube was renovated in 2007 by the university's Department of Capital Projects's design group as the new home for the Department of Anthropology. The symmetrical north elevation, politely aligned with the Central Steam Plant to the east, presents a matching pair of recessed entrances on Russell Street, which are lined with sculpted blue and white ceramic units that mark the building as a child of the early 1960s. Between the two entries is a bronze sculpture, based on cedar trees, by the noted Canadian artist Walter Yarwood.

The most engaging architectural aspect of the building occurs at its inverted corners, where a splayed detail carefully exposes and articulates the brick cladding. Viewed from below, these corners read as "negative columns."

49. Central Steam Plant *Gordon Adamson & Associates, 1952*
Addition *1960*

The Central Steam Plant blends in so well with its surroundings that it is easy to walk by and miss its simple but powerful modernity. Ten enormous windows articulated with thin sash bars command the north facade, revealing the functional apparatus inside. At the main entrance, steel-framed glazing wraps smartly around the plant's northwest corner. The Central Steam Plant's most sublime moment occurs in the rear service yard, where, at the base of the building's monumental concrete stack, a composition of giant twisting ducts inspire genuine awe.

Cody Hall

50. Cody Hall (Department of Astronomy and Astrophysics) *Allward & Gouinlock Architects, 1953*

Cody Hall, named in honor of university president Canon Henry Cody (1932–45), was originally the university's School of Nursing. In retrospect, its location can be seen as a quiet but important factor in the university's aggressive westward expansion during the 1960s. In 1956 President Smith stated in a letter that "in placing the Heating Plant [Central Steam Plant] and the School of Nursing west of St. George Street we have, in effect, made the decision to go west."

With its humanely scaled elevations, the building anchors the northwest corner of St. George and Russell streets well, and many original materials and detailing survive in the main interior spaces. Surprisingly, conservative Cody Hall was designed by architects Allward & Gouinlock just five years after they completed the overtly modern Mechanical Engineering building on King's College Road (see page 74). Had they lost confidence in modernism, or were they simply the kind of firm that was adroit at working in a variety of styles? Whatever was the case, by the early 1960s Allward & Gouinlock Architects were once again in the modernist camp, as evidenced by their design for the Lash Miller Chemical Laboratories.

Lash Miller Chemical Laboratories

51. Lash Miller Chemical Laboratories and the John and Edna Davenport Chemical Research Building

Lash Miller Chemical Laboratories *Allward & Gouinlock Architects, 1963*

John and Edna Davenport Chemical Research Laboratories *Diamond + Schmitt Architects, 2001*

Davenport Chemical Research Building/Lash Miller Chemical Laboratories Garden *Phillips Farevaag Smallenberg in association with PMA Landscape Architects, 2005*

The Lash Miller Chemical Laboratories originally comprised three components: a block-long, seven-story volume paralleling Willcocks Street; a one-story lecture hall at the corner of Willcocks and St. George streets; and a two-story wing along St. George street. The building's main section is clad in brown brick with a regular rhythm of windows framed by aquamarine steel panels below. Carefully designed areas of small aquamarine ceramic tiles provide secondary articulation on the energetic front entrance canopy's soffit and in a somewhat wacky "Swiss-cheese-roofed" garden element to the west that hides exhaust ducts. On the exterior of the concrete lecture hall, the building announces its function through a display of three-dimensional chemical symbols.

A decade ago, a major addition to the building, the John and Edna Davenport Chemical Research Laboratories, was constructed atop the two-story wing along St. George Street. Using sympathetic materials and scale, the architects success-fully blended new and old. The glass-enclosed, cantilevered stair at the addition's south end and the copper-clad, bowed-out element on its west facade give exuber-ance to the revitalized ensemble.

Like other buildings in the area such as the McLennan Physical Laboratories and Sidney Smith Hall, the chemistry building complex has deep moats running along most of its edges in order to bring natural light to the basement level. While not particularly attractive or friendly, some of the moats have nevertheless been imaginatively incorporated into the new garden between the Lash Miller Chemical Laboratories, the Davenport Chemical Research Building, and the McLennan Physical Laboratories.

Burton Tower, McLennan Physical Laboratories

52. McLennan Physical Laboratories
Shore & Moffat & Partners, 1967

Now more than forty years old, the fourteen-story Burton Tower and three-story wing to its north that constitute the McLennan Physical Laboratories are starting to feel historic, and certain aspects of this 1960s architecture are quite captivating. At first glance, the tower and its wing seem a bit brutish, and an insistent moat that wraps around the complex adds to their standoffish appearance. However, closer examina-tion reveals a highly disciplined, if spare, architecture.

Earth Sciences Centre and Bancroft Avenue

Sitting on a small elevated plaza, the tower is clad in stone and charcoal-brown brick, with glazing areas that are broken into nicely proportioned horizontal bands (which are repeated, in various subcompositions, throughout the project). Square in plan, the tower reveals its structural bays—four on each side—with cantilevered corners. Inside visitors can view North America's first electronic microscope, from 1938.

53. Earth Sciences Centre

Bregman + Hamann Architects/A. J. Diamond, Donald Schmitt and Company, 1989

High Bay Facility *Barry–Bryan Associates, 2002*

In the mid-1970s, the university announced intentions to construct a major facility for the departments of botany, forestry, geography, geology, and environmental studies. After more than a decade of planning, the 100,000-square-foot (9290-square-meter) Earth Sciences Centre, consuming half the large urban block bounded by Willcocks, Huron, and Russell streets, was finally realized. Although architecturally of its time, it does not look outdated today, twenty years after its opening, partly because it was designed to dissolve into the surrounding urban fabric. Several existing historic buildings were preserved and integrated into the project.

The center is organized around two major axes: a north-south axis, expressed as a covered colonnade; and an east-west axis, consisting of pedestrianized

Graduate Students' Union

Bancroft Avenue. Adjacent to the intersection of the axes is a five-story ellipti-cal volume containing an auditorium, library, and reading room. Laboratories, classrooms, and offices are housed in linked linear buildings that form hard urban edges along Willcocks, Huron, and Russell streets. The naturalized concept for a series of outdoor courtyards came from the landscape architect Michael Hough, aided by the expertise of the botany and forestry faculty and serving some of their research interests. At the heart of the Earth Sciences Centre is Bancroft Avenue, formerly a vehicular route connecting Huron Street to Spadina Avenue. Architects Jack Diamond and Donald Schmitt transformed this street into an elongated urban space that now functions like a piazza.

The building's architecture speaks with a highly contextual, postmodern voice, employing steeply gabled planes, a variety of materials, and captivating bands of ocular windows that hover somewhere between Georgian and porthole-Moderne. The motifs and particular use of color and materials in the Earth Sciences Centre are highly abstracted, however, distinguishing this postmodern project from the saccharine overkill that too frequently occurred during the 1970s and 1980s.

54. Graduate Students' Union *Gordon & Helliwell, 1911*

This small, spirited building was originally a private club, the Baraca Club, and at one time contained a swimming pool and a bowling alley, along with an open yard to its east, bordering the City (later Borden) Dairy service garage. The former club now houses the Graduate Students' Union, its pub, and the Sylvester's Cafe. Large wooden brackets support an overhanging roof, and two graceful bay windows mark the lower front facade of the building.

55. Koffler Building *Shore Tilbe Henschel Irwin Peters, 1990*
Multi-faith Centre for Spiritual Study and Practice *Moriyama & Teshima Architects, 2007*

Located at the west end of Bancroft Avenue, this postmodern structure was designed to house the Koffler Institute for Pharmacy Management, which moved in 2006 to the new Leslie L. Dan Pharmacy Building several blocks to the southeast. Architects Shore Tilbe Henschel Irwin Peters achieved a low-key contextualism by relating the institute's height and materials to nearby historic buildings and by gently curving its Spadina Avenue–facing facade toward Spadina Crescent and the Borden Buildings to the south. Sculptural orange-tan and yellow brick walls dance in and out, up and down. The building's design creates some surprising and exuberant moments—for example, at the upper northwest corner, the third-floor volume is indented to make a triangular space, into which juts a triangular bay window. Entering the building from Bancroft Avenue, one is immediately inside a soaring, light-filled rotunda space, topped by a curved dome and accented with bands of glass block. Its verticality is exaggerated by eight slender concrete columns that rise through the full three stories and support a ring of balconies.

Recently, the 6,000-square-foot (550-square-meter) Multi-faith Centre for Spiritual Study and Practice was skillfully inserted into the building. Using a restrained palette of bare concrete, white onyx, and sapele (an African hardwood), Moriyama & Teshima Architects created a handsome sequence of sacred spaces appropriate for all faiths. The center's focus is a large meeting space that can be transformed into prayer and lecture areas. A small meditation room features a "living wall" of air-cleansing plants. Even the storage areas for religious tools and iconography—Buddhist scrolls, Christian crosses, Jewish Torahs, First Nations sweetgrass—are elegantly designed.

56. Faculty Club *Benjamin Brown, 1920*

This Georgian-revival building started life as the Cosmopolitan Club, before it became the Primrose Club, an elite Jewish men's club. (Women were eventually admitted.) Its designer was Benjamin Brown, one of Toronto's first Jewish architects, who was responsible for the design of several landmarks in the city, including the Beth Jacob Synagogue (1922), the Balfour Building (1930), and the extremely

TOP: *Koffler Building*

BOTTOM: *Multi-faith Centre for Spiritual Study and Practice*

interesting Hermant Office Tower (1929), which stands at the southeast corner of Dundas Square.

In 1959 the university's faculty union obtained the building, leading to the formation of the present-day Faculty Club. When the neighboring New College Residence was constructed in 2003, the Faculty Club created a delightful outdoor dining terrace along the west side of their building.

Faculty Club

57. New College Residence *Saucier + Perrotte, 2003*

This is the third student residence constructed for New College, joining New College I (Wetmore Hall) and New College II (Wilson Hall), which are located directly to the north across Willcocks Street (see Walk Five). The nine-story "new New College," as the 2003 building is known, provides single-room accommodations for 277 students. It blends admirably into its physical setting, responding, chameleonlike, to its urban and immediate campus contexts.

The residence hall is made up of two parallel "bar" buildings with service cores between. The west-facing bar, along Spadina Avenue, is clad in red brick and has a staccato pattern of white-framed windows. A cubic void is cut into the bar, generating an outdoor garden room. The building relates comfortably to the small-scale, red brick Victorian houses in the neighborhood across the street. The east-facing bar, which faces the university, is clad in zinc and has larger, regularly spaced windows. It also incorporates a cubic garden, which is reminiscent of the residential gardens in the sky favored by Le Corbusier. The residence's main entrance is tucked under and between the bars along Willcocks Street, where the differentiated conceptual logic of the two bar facades is momentarily revealed.

Between the New College Residence, the Faculty Club, and the Graduate Students' Union, a public pedestrian walkway, a dining terrace, and a courtyard announce the rear, campus-side entrance to the building. Underneath the unadorned lobbies, the architects inserted a beautifully proportioned multipurpose hall, the William Doo Auditorium.

New College Residence

58. North and South Borden Buildings *George M. Miller*
North Building *1900*
South Building *1910*

The North and South Borden Buildings are currently run down and neglected, but they have interesting histories as part of a complex of buildings that housed the City Dairy, which was owned by the Massey family, ambitious supporters of pasteurized milk production. The Dentonia Park Farm, a model dairy farm owned by the Masseys and also designed by George M. Miller, supplied raw milk to the City Dairy, which was purchased by the Toronto division of the Borden Company, Ltd. around 1940.

The large North Building contained production areas for butter and milk, cold storage, offices, and employee dressing rooms, while the South Building was devoted to ice cream making. Walking under the second-floor enclosed passageway that connects the two buildings, one discovers an outdoor service court, which, with its old brick walls on two sides and antiquated loading docks, still conveys a strong sense of history and place. The Borden Buildings now accommodate various university offices and centers, including the central mail room, the Centre for Women and Trans People, the Centre for Aboriginal Initiatives, and a First Nations House with a birch bark canoe suspended from its third-floor ceiling.

Unfortunately, the pair of red brick buildings has suffered some mindless renovations, including the filling in of two bays of the once lovely five-bay front porch of

North and South Borden Buildings

the North Building. Nevertheless, the upper portion of this curved-front building still conveys a sense of grandeur through its two-story engaged brick columns. Seen today, the Borden Buildings are more noteworthy from an urban standpoint than for their architecture. Their stage-set-like front facades help shape the northeast portion of Spadina Crescent, the large traffic circle in the center of Spadina Avenue. Still, the scenographic buildings could play an even stronger role in the campus's appearance and deserve to be imaginatively rethought and rehabilitated.

59. One Spadina Crescent *Smith & Gemmell, 1875*
Master plan *Kuwabara Payne McKenna Blumberg Architects, 2007*

Among the places that clearly stand out in the 1878 color lithograph *Bird's-Eye View of Toronto* (see page 10) is the Presbyterian Theological School of Knox College, not only because it was a city landmark at the time, but also because it commands a unique circular piece of land right in the center of Spadina Avenue. Knox College moved to King's College Circle in 1915, and after that its old building became the Spadina Military Hospital for World War One veterans. It was sold to Connaught Laboratories in 1943, and the university purchased it in 1972. One Spadina Crescent has since hosted many users, including the Department of Ophthalmology, the Eye Bank of Canada, the Department of Anthropology, the

One Spadina Crescent

Department of Art's visual studies program, and overflow from the architecture department.

The prominence of the building's site has attracted numerous development proposals over the years, some quite grandiose. At the end of the 1920s, when the Toronto Maple Leafs' owner Conn Smythe was deciding where to construct a new arena for his team, he and a group of businessmen proposed to tear down the existing building at Spadina Crescent and erect a sixteen-thousand-seat circular hockey arena, architecturally similar to the Olympic Arena in Detroit. But this grand notion did not fly, and in 1931 the Maple Leafs built their new home on Carleton Street instead.

Now the historically designated neo-Gothic building is slated for restoration and expansion. As one of Toronto's most fanciful structures to survive from the Victorian era, One Spadina Crescent deserves to recover its former architectural splendor.

WALK FIVE: THE NORTHWEST CAMPUS

BLOOR STREET WEST

67

66

65

64

63

62

ST. GEORGE STREET

HARBORD STREET

61

60

WILLCOCKS STREET

BACK CAMPUS

FRONT CAMPUS

Walk Five: The Northwest Campus

About a third of the University of Toronto's northwest campus consists of shady, quiet streets lined with Victorian-style houses from the late nineteenth and early twentieth centuries, nearly 80 percent of which are owned by the university and used for academic purposes or rented to students or faculty. This pocket of tranquility has largely survived despite aggressive growth in the mid-twentieth century, when both the university and the city had grandiose plans for the area.

In the 1950s and 1960s, the university did demolish entire residential blocks through eminent domain to allow the construction of huge projects such as Sidney Smith Hall (1961) and the John P. Robarts Research Library (1968–73) on the northwest campus. In the mid-1960s, the city announced plans for the north-south Spadina Expressway, which was to extend down Spadina Road and Spadina Avenue, making a noisy wall of speeding traffic along the university's western edge. Following grassroots protests led by Jane Jacobs, the famous planning critic who had recently moved from New York City to Toronto, and supported by civic leaders, downtown residents, and academics such as Marshall McLuhan, further construction of the Spadina Expressway south of Eglinton Avenue was stopped in the summer of 1971. Walking along Spadina Avenue today, one can still see traces of reactions to the once impending expressway: some of the university's buildings from the 1960s, such as New College, turned their backs to the street as a defense against it.

In recent years, the university has further densified the northwest campus with projects such as Graduate House, the Early Learning Centre, the School of Continuing Studies, and the Department of Economics. These new constructions, which often incorporate existing buildings, promise to preserve much of the northwest campus as the special, peaceful enclave that it has been for more than a century.

Sidney Smith Hall

60. Sidney Smith Hall

John B. Parkin Associates, 1961
South addition *Beinhaker/Irwin Associates, mid-1980s*
Infill and renovation *Ian MacDonald Architect, Inc., 2002 and 2004*

In 1956 the University of Toronto's Plateau Committee, set up by President Sidney Smith, set out to double the university's enrollment, from twelve thousand to

Sidney Smith Hall

twenty-four thousand students. Soon after, a 1957 master planning committee proposed that "a centrally located arts building should be built on the west side of St. George Street" as part of the university's new west campus, leading to the construction of Sidney Smith Hall, named for the university's sixth president, who later became Canada's secretary of state for external affairs. The hall, known as "Sid Smith," houses the Faculty of Arts and Science, which has more than twenty-five thousand students, making it the largest academic division in the university.

Opened in 1961, the building was uncompromisingly modern, consisting of a long, six-story slab with large windows; a floating, solid-looking volume extending southward from the slab structure; and two expansive concrete terraces to the east and west. Following the dictates of the west campus master plan, these elements were set on a plinth, to provide a basement service level with some natural lighting. The building—whose concrete structure was clad in stone, precast concrete, and brick—was a mid-twentieth-century essay on the flow of space and light. None of this seems radical now, but at the time Sid Smith was a trailblazer at the university, since the only other overtly modernist buildings on campus were the 1948 addition to the Mechanical Engineering Building, the Central Steam Plant of 1952, the Women's Athletic Building of 1959, and 215 Huron Street (Superintendent's Building), also opened in 1959.

Sid Smith has been added to, renovated, and infilled over the years, forfeiting its stylistic purity but at the same time reducing the building's aloofness. With the addition of broad steps, the elevated terraces are now visually and socially integrated with the public sidewalks. Thoughtful infill projects by Ian MacDonald Architect, Inc., in 2002 and 2004, clad in corrugated stainless steel, have brought metallic sparkle to the building in the form of light-filled student lounges and meeting spaces.

LEFT: *Ramsay Wright Zoological Laboratories*
RIGHT: *John P. Robarts Research Library, detail of facade*

61. Ramsay Wright Zoological Laboratories
Marani Morris & Allan, 1965
Centre for Biological Timing and Cognition *Stantec Inc., 2007*

The Department of Zoology grew out of the Department of Biology and was established in 1916 by Robert Ramsay Wright, a noted biologist and the university's first vice-president. The building named to honor him, known simply as "Ramsay Wright," is one of the largest on the northwest campus, but its architecture is unremarkable. With the exception of its confidently expressed stair towers, everything about it is so neutral that one can pass the building day after day and easily ignore it. Its primary, T-shaped volume runs east-west from St. George Street to Huron Street, with the north side and main lobby facing a lawn that runs along Harbord Street. An awkwardly shaped pavilion, linked to the main building and containing lecture halls and offices, is situated at the key intersection of Harbord and St. George streets.

The 1965 complex is happily offset by two more recent projects: the silvery green Centre for Biological Timing and Cognition addition at Ramsay Wright's southwest corner and a zoomorphic sculpture of a moose, titled *Mooseconstrue,* installed on a grassy hill at the building's northeast corner by artist Charles Pachter. It is the cutout positive of the "negative" moose sculpture Pachter made for the courtyard at nearby Graduate House.

62. John P. Robarts Research Library, Thomas Fisher Rare Book Library, and the Claude T. Bissell Building (Faculty of Information)
Warner, Burns, Toan & Lunde (design consultants) with Mathers & Haldenby (architects), 1971–73
Master plan for renewal and expansion *Diamond + Schmitt Architects, 2008*

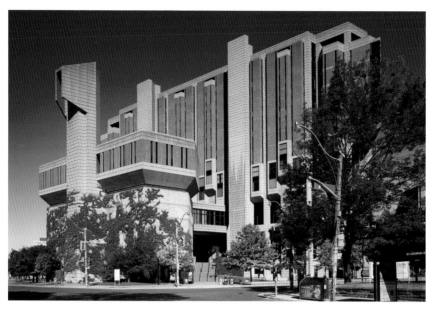

John P. Robarts Research Library and Thomas Fisher Rare Book Library

The John P. Robarts Research Library complex presents itself as a modern monument, rising above and peering over the campus. As the institution's "treasury of knowledge," it has an unambiguous architectural authority appropriate to its role.

With 9.6 million items, the Robarts Research Library is the largest book repository in Canada. It is the main humanities and social sciences library of the University of Toronto Library (UTL) system, which is the third largest academic library system in North America after those at Harvard and Yale. Even with the recent creation of a warehouse depository off-campus, though, the library has become inadequate for today's university of more than 70,000 students, and a new master plan was launched in 2008.

By February of 1962, the university took the first steps to the library complex when it launched plans to add to the existing library on King's College Circle. Architects Mathers & Haldenby had produced preliminary sketches for an extension eastward and a square, seven-story tower to replace the much older portions of the library. Their proposal went no further, however, due to cost, space, and time issues. Instead, then-President Claude Bissell persuaded the Ontario Ministry of University Affairs to make available a new, much larger site: an entire city block bounded by St. George Street, Sussex Avenue, Huron Street, and Harbord Street. Bissell decided the new library would be the university's showstopping Canadian centennial project for 1967—even if it meant clearing the block of houses by eminent domain. A library school was added to the program, and in March 1964, Mathers & Haldenby presented a feasibility study for the new site "in the form of a six-storey rectangle running parallel to St. George Street, set on a broad podium." (It is little known that just one month later, John Andrews, the architect and

University of Toronto professor who had designed Scarborough College, put forward a design for the library formed like a large amphitheatre. Although not carried forward, Andrews's unorthodox proposal did propel President Bissell and the newly formed Library Committee in more exciting directions.)

In 1966 the Library Committee, led by Robert H. Blackburn, went on a tour of six libraries in the United States, two of which were designed by the New York firm of Warner, Burns, Toan & Lunde (WBTL), which led to the university's decision to commission WBTL in association with Mathers & Haldenby. From the five different designs generated by WBTL, a scheme based on triangular geometry was chosen, both because it could provide a window in each of the one-thousand study carrel rooms the program called for and because President Bissell wanted something bold and exciting.

Constructed of poured-in-place and precast concrete, the central Robarts Research Library rises fourteen stories, flanked by two lower volumes: the Fisher Rare Book Library at the southeast and the Faculty of Information Studies (now the Faculty of Information) at the northeast. The gray concrete exterior contrasts with warmer finishes inside, including African mahogany from Ghana. The use of wood is especially effective in the soaring central space of the rare book facility, which, in its moody darkness, is one of the most astonishing spaces on campus. The building's triangulated geometry is sometimes frustrating: climbing the strangely angular main entrance steps is a chore. But at other times, moving up through the library—through hexagonal and octagonal spaces and, finally, to rooms in the pointed prows that jut from the upper levels—is genuinely exhilarating.

When it opened in the early 1970s, the library complex was met by some with great hostility—it was even likened to George Orwell's Ministry of Truth. Architect Ron Thom, designer of nearby Massey College, called it an "illustrated dictionary of architectural miseries," and scathing reviews appear even today. What can finally be deduced from this storm of provocation? Why does the Robarts Research Library spawn so much virulence? Perhaps its monumentality and slightly spooky "otherness" are the causes. It stands alone, proud, and aloof, serving as a harsh reminder of our miniscule place in the grand scheme of things—something we would generally prefer to forget.

63. Innis College
A. J. Diamond & Barton Myers (designed by A. J. Diamond), 1975

Founded in 1964, Innis College, which offers a multidisciplinary program, is named for Harold Innis, who was a prominent University of Toronto political economist. With around 1,650 students, Innis is a small community, and its main building, finished in 1975, is similarly scaled. The structure is an early example of architect

LEFT: *Innis College*
RIGHT: *Max Gluskin House*

Jack Diamond's expertise with renovation, urban infill, and the creation of courtyard spaces, evident in Toronto projects such as Beverley Place (see page 249) and his firm's Bahen Centre for Information Technology and Earth Sciences Centre.

Innis College consists of a renovated Victorian house and a series of linked orange brick-clad additions that match the rhythm and scale of the nineteenth-century streetscapes along Sussex Avenue and St. George Street. These house-like volumes are interrupted by entrance areas with fully glazed roofs, making Innis College one of the brightest and most cheerful interior environments on campus. On the north and west sides, the building opens to a pleasant outdoor courtyard, now further enhanced by the adjoining courtyard of Max Gluskin House. The heart of Innis College is the Town Hall, a well-proportioned room that serves as a forum and also functions as a fully equipped cinema. In 1994 the college added a residence hall for its students directly across St. George Street.

64. Max Gluskin House (Department of Economics)
Hariri Pontarini Architects, 2008
150 St. George Street *architect unknown, 1889*
South wing *Allward & Gouinlock Architects, 1960*

Recently completed as the home of the Department of Economics, Max Gluskin House efficiently links two restored historic buildings facing St. George Street with a new L-shaped wing along the north and west edges of the site. This complex, designed by Hariri Pontarini Architects, focuses on a sunny, south-facing courtyard. The old-plus-new strategy, and the resulting sophistication and warmth of the architecture, are reminiscent of Woodsworth College (1991) directly across the street, which architect Siamak Hariri was also involved with.

The oldest part of Max Gluskin House is the Victorian home built in 1889 for William Crowther, a partner in the firm of wholesale grocers Sloan & Crowther. In 1927 the house and a coach house at the rear were acquired by the China Inland Mission, an international organization formed to spread Christianity throughout China. They added a structure at the back of the house and connected it at the second level to the coach house, allowing a driveway to pass underneath. The Canadian Medical Association purchased the site in 1955 and in 1960 completed a flat-roofed, Georgian revival-style wing to the south. The complex was taken over by the university in the 1960s to house its Centre for Urban and Community Studies and, later, the Institute for Policy Analysis, before the Department of Economics moved into the building in 1982.

In composing the new Max Gluskin House complex on the constrained site, Hariri Pontarini Architects first performed some creative erasure, demolishing the coach house and eliminating the driveway. The two northern bays of the 1960s addition were torn down, opening up breathing room and providing transparency between the Victorian and Georgian-revival pieces. Now the St. George Street facade has a pleasing rhythm of old-new-old-new. Also noteworthy are the robust Cor-ten steel panels on the courtyard facades and the rugged brickwork on the wing along the western edge of the site, where Max Gluskin House meets bpNichol Lane.

65. Coach House Books *c. 1890, architect unknown*

Coach House Books

The Coach House Books publishing house was founded in 1965 by Stan Bevington and has occupied a series of old coach houses on bpNichol Lane since 1968. It produces innovative and experimental books with small print runs that larger publishers would not take on and has published works by such illustrious figures as Margaret Atwood, bpNichol, Allen Ginsberg, and Michael Ondaatje. One of bpNichol's poems appears on the concrete lane alongside Coach House Books's offices, reading, "A LAKE, A LANE, A LINE, A LONE." Although Coach House Books is not part of the university, this tiny place is such a literary landmark and so much a part of the northwest campus community that it would be wrong not to include it here. In 2008 the publisher won the Ontario Premier's Award for Excellence in the Arts.

School of Continuing Studies

66. School of Continuing Studies *Robert M. Saunders, 1958*
Renovation and addition *Moriyama & Teshima Architects, 2004*

In the 1970s, the university transformed its former Department of Extension into
the School of Continuing Studies. The school grew rapidly and now offers hundreds of courses and certificate programs to more than fifteen thousand people
annually. To accommodate the expanding program, a preexisting modern office

building, which was originally the St. George Medical Centre, was completely over-hauled by Moriyama & Teshima Architects. They added a two-story, glass-enclosed "living room" to the front to welcome people and connect with the community. This cubic room has a trellised sunshade wrapping around the east facade and the southeast corner, where it intersects a freestanding wall of stone. The most intriguing space in the renovated building is the double-height lounge-seminar room at its west end, where three unusual slit windows provide subdued natural light: a low horizontal one overlooks a tiny garden; a vertical one looks to the west; and a north-facing horizontal window opens to the sky.

67. Jackman Humanities Building
Marani, Lawson & Paisley, 1929
Jackman Humanities Institute *Kohn Shnier Architects, 2008*

Jackman Humanities Building

The university purchased this build-ing in 2002 for use as teaching, research, and office space, and recently named it in honor of Hal Jackman, the twenty-fifth lieuten-ant governor of Ontario and former chancellor of the university. The ten-story structure, designed by architects Marani, Lawson & Paisley in 1929, combines Georgian and Moderne influences in a stepped form reminiscent of Manhattan sky-scrapers of the era.

Although the Jackman Humanities Building, seen from Bloor and St. George streets, appears to be a huge, four-square block, it is actually L-shaped. Its more visible east and west sides are dressed in Indiana limestone and fully decorated, while the rest of the exterior is more plain-looking. The main lobby off St. George Street is decked out in bronze and *verde antique* marble and embellished with fancy lighting fixtures. Practicality was also important to the architects, who incor-porated state-of-the-art Otis-Fensom elevators, telephone systems, laundry chutes, and compressed-air distribution systems into the design.

Kohn Shnier Architects transformed the tenth-floor penthouse into the Jackman Humanities Institute in 2008, and, with the 1929 lobby, it is one of the showpiece spaces in the building. Envisioned as a "Circle of Fellows," the institute will bring together scholars from all the humanities branches, including architecture, fine arts, philosophy, and literature.

LEFT: *University of Toronto Schools*
RIGHT: *Studio Theatre*

68. University of Toronto Schools (UTS)

Darling & Pearson, 1910
Auditorium and east wing *1924*
First west wing *1931*
Second west wing *Marani & Morris, 1949*
Spadina wing *Marani & Morris, 1958*
Spadina wing renovations *DuBois Plumb Partnership, 1999*

University of Toronto Schools (UTS) was planned in the early twentieth century
as a one-thousand-pupil model school with two hundred teachers. It was to serve
primary and secondary students (both boys and girls) and would include a technical school. When funding was not available for this ambitious plan, the technical
school and lower primary grades were eliminated, and enrollment was limited to
boys. (Girls were eventually admitted, starting in 1973.) Although the original grand
vision was never implemented, UTS expanded numerous times over its hundred-
year history. The school had a glorious start, followed by a gradual diminishment
of spatial and material aspirations. Between 1910 and 1958, its architecture went
from being inspiring to merely functional.

The original, bilaterally symmetrical building, designed by Darling & Pearson
and facing Bloor Street West, mirrored the ideals of the Faculty of Education,
which set out in 1910 to establish a model environment for practice teaching. The

building was (and still is) dignified, proud, and robust. The very first issue of the *UTS Monthly*, from February 1920, has a perspective drawing of the Georgian-revival brick building on the cover, revealing its architectural and institutional authority.

Over the years, UTS evolved into an E-shaped structure with a fine eight-hundred-seat auditorium at its center. Directly above is the library, whose furnishings and character have changed little since 1910. Equally interesting is the tiny gymnasium on the first floor, stacked above a ground-floor swimming pool, both part of the 1924 addition.

By the time wings were added in 1949 and 1958, Darling & Pearson were no longer involved, architectural ambitions had been ratcheted down considerably, and no-frills functionality prevailed. However, in 1999 the second and third floors of the west wing were renovated by DuBois Plumb Partnership, who provided handsome quarters for the university's Department of Sociology, signaling a reaffirmation of the original commitment to quality architecture established at UTS a century ago.

69. Studio Theatre *Maurice Klein, 1914*
Renovations *late 1960s*

This former church houses the Graduate Centre for the Study of Drama and includes a one hundred-seat "black box" theater. Originally St. Paul's Lutheran English Church, the building was designed by architect Maurice Klein, who was just seventeen years old when he signed the building permit for the church in 1913. From the 1930s to the 1960s, the church served a Russian Orthodox congregation. Following deconsecration in 1966, it was sold to the university.

Tyrone Guthrie, first artistic director at the Shakespeare Festival Theatre in Stratford, Ontario, and founder of the Guthrie Theater in Minneapolis, Minnesota, was subsequently invited to the university to comment on the possibility of making the former church into a theater. The idea gained momentum and, following renovations, the Studio Theatre opened on October 16, 1968.

70. Graduate House
Morphosis/Teeple Architects, Inc. (joint venture), 2000

In the 1990s, the University of Toronto decided to significantly expand residential space for students on the St. George campus, given both the high cost of renting an apartment in downtown Toronto and the desire of the University of Toronto to create a stronger sense of community. Graduate House was the first building planned under that initiative, on a constricted site bounded by Harbord Street,

Graduate House

Spadina Avenue, and Glen Morris Street. The city imposed height restrictions and also required a publicly accessible courtyard. The university and the School of Graduate Studies further increased expectations by calling for a student-oriented cafe at the new building's southwest corner and asking that it act as a "gateway" into the campus from the west.

An international, by-invitation competition in 1998 was won by Los Angeles–based architecture firm Morphosis in joint venture with Toronto's Teeple Architects, Inc. Their aggressively deconstructivist design generated immediate controversy, especially the proposed monumental gateway cantilever over Harbord Street, which Thom Mayne of Morphosis referred to as a "Pop-scale, two-story cornice." The cantilever's "borrowing" of public space over the sidewalk and street was what caused the biggest row, but the city strongly supported the project. Graduate House opened in 2000, and architecture critic Christopher Hume christened it Toronto's "first architectural landmark of the twenty-first century."

The dramatic building consists of efficient urban blocks composed around a central courtyard and reflecting pool, the latter graced by a humorous Cor-ten steel moose sculpture by artist Charles Pachter. Graduate House is clad in charcoal-colored precast concrete with a perforated aluminum skin draped over the north and east facades. A skew in the south block generates positive agitation and "delaminates" the facade into overlapping planes of texture. The tight packing of the structure accommodates over 420 graduate students in 120 apartment-type suites. Two-story units in the east wing are interlocked in section, similar to Le Corbusier's Unité d'Habitation (1946–52) in Marseille, France. The utopian approaches to housing that infiltrate this project seem to flow from a broad range of early-twentieth-century sources, including that of the Russian avant-garde. For example, Graduate House shares a certain kinship with the Narkomfin Housing project in Moscow (1928–29) by Moisei Ginsburg. But it is the dramatically cantilevered tectonic element hovering over Harbord Street—simultaneously cornice, corridor, lounge, gateway, and sign—that gives the building its signature status. Here, "University of Toronto" is spelled out in giant ceramic-frit lettering on glass. (The final sculptural "O" is made of steel.)

Graduate House is a strong forerunner of later Morphosis buildings, such as the Caltrans District 7 Headquarters Building in Los Angeles, where overlapping planes and skins give the building an ethereal character. Graduate House went on to win design awards from *Canadian Architect*, *Progressive Architecture,* and the Los Angeles chapter of the American Institute of Architects, and in 2005 Thom Mayne won the prestigious Pritzker Prize.

Early Learning Centre

71. Early Learning Centre *Teeple Architects, Inc., 2003*

Silvery and sculptural, this day-care facility for one hundred children is a little gem. It primarily accommodates the children of University of Toronto faculty, staff, and students, from infants to junior kindergarten age. The center's three levels of integrated indoor-outdoor learning and playing areas are organized around a dramatic ramp that extends from the east-side car-arrival and drop-off area to the second floor. Vertical slots thread through the structure, bringing natural light deep into the building and generating exaggerated views from one level to another. The experience of moving through the building is like climbing in a giant, fantastic tree house.

72. Clara Benson Building *Fleury, Arthur & Barclay, 1959*

The Clara Benson Building, originally known as the Women's Athletic Building, is part of the group of mid-twentieth-century buildings known locally as "Toronto Modern." Indeed, its embrace of modernism was radical for Toronto in 1959. Built tight to the surrounding sidewalks, it had a surprising urbanity at a time when the university seemed to think of the new west campus with a suburban mentality.

Clad in brown bricks that range in color, the building's structural frame is periodically

Clara Benson Building

exposed, faced in tiny white and beige-gold ceramic tiles. Its structure is easily readable at the top of the long east elevation, and a varied pattern of fenestration suggests the functional layout of the athletic facilities within. At the southeast corner are projecting balconies, the south-facing one enlivened by a three-bay scalloped concrete canopy.

Clara Benson, the building's namesake, was a powerhouse at the University of Toronto for fifty years. She received a doctorate degree in chemistry from the university in 1903 (one of the first two women in Toronto to be awarded one), and from 1926 to 1945 was head of the Department of Food Chemistry in the Lillian Massey Department of Household Science. During World War Two, she set up a course that taught women in munitions factories how to measure the chemical properties of explosives. The Clara Benson Building was named to recognize her efforts to obtain better athletic facilities for female students. In 1998 it was linked to and integrated with the Warren Stevens Building to the west to create a larger, more flexible athletic center.

73. Warren Stevens Building

Prack & Prack (later Norman Dobell Associates Architects), 1979
Renovations *Oleson Worland Architects, 1998*

Warren Stevens Building

The Warren Stevens Building embodies the definition of "athletic": it seems physically powerful and large and muscular in build. In fact, no other building on the St.George campus has the sheer sense of mass displayed by this building, known as "Fort Jock." Proudly exposing its tons of reinforced-concrete structure, this monolithic hulk has plenty of architectural presence, its seriousness only contested by the smiling rounded corners of its red steel window frames. To accommodate the enormous clear-span spaces necessary for a fifty-meter Olympic-size pool and a five-lane two-hundred-meter indoor running track (the largest in Ontario), the building has a superstructure of four huge steel trusses, each twenty-two feet deep, that carry loads to the corners of the building, where concrete piers transfer them to deep foundations.

The Warren Stevens Building is a modernist "machine," supporting athletic, fitness, and recreational activities. However, its internalized nature causes it to ignore the surrounding streets, particularly busy Spadina Avenue. The recent addition of a coffee shop and outdoor cafe facing Harbord Street is a first positive step toward softening the building's urban edges.

New College

74. New College

North building (New College I/Wetmore Hall) *Fairfield & DuBois, 1964*
South building (New College II/Wilson Hall) *Fairfield & DuBois, 1969*
Addition and renovation *Dunker Associates, 1999*

Founded in 1962, New College consists of three structures: a pair of flowing, spatially interlocking buildings from the 1960s designed by Macy DuBois of Fairfield & DuBois, and a residence hall completed in 2003. The two older buildings owe a debt to the Finnish architect Alvar Aalto, who influenced DuBois. The imaginative, thoughtfully designed complex immediately recalls Aalto's masterful, curvilinear Baker House dormitory at MIT of 1948. There are subtle differences between the north and south buildings, which were finished five years apart. The north building, Wetmore Hall, has rectangular columns and features a series of concrete fins along the upper ribbon windows, and also seems less refined than the later south building, Wilson Hall. This structure has round columns, no upper concrete fins, and metal-slat ceilings in its main public areas. Both buildings use robust materials—brick, slate, wood—and have lovely period lighting fixtures, including the huge orange cylindrical lights in the D. G. Ivey Library in Wilson Hall.

DuBois gave the buildings logical, rectilinear facades along their street- and sidewalk-facing edges, contrasting these hard sides with soft, flowing facades facing inward, creating an interior S-shaped courtyard.

WALK SIX:

THE MEDICAL AND HEALTH SCIENCES DISTRICT

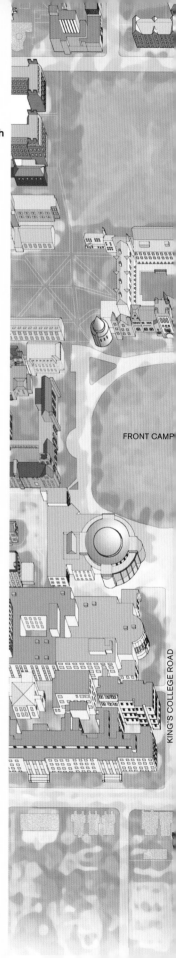

FRONT CAMP

KING'S COLLEGE ROAD

QUEEN'S PARK

QUEEN'S PARK CRESCENT WEST

QUEEN'S PARK CRESCENT EAST

PROVINCIAL LEGISLATURE

75

76

78

79

77

84

83

85

80

81

82

COLLEGE STREET

UNIVERSITY AVENUE

86

87

Walk Six: The Medical and Health Sciences District

The University of Toronto's faculties of medicine, nursing, dentistry, and pharmacy are within a fifteen-minute walk of one another, threaded in and around the southeast corner of the downtown campus. Known as "Toronto's Discovery District," this area includes University Avenue, which is lined with major hospitals, and is also the locus of the city's expanding biomedical industry, symbolized by the dynamic MaRS Centre.

Unlike universities such as Northwestern and Harvard that operate teaching hospitals and have easily identified medical precincts, the University of Toronto does not own or run any hospitals. Furthermore, only a few of the twenty-seven hospitals and centers affiliated with the university's health sciences programs are geographically within the Walk Six zone. Most are scattered throughout downtown Toronto, the suburbs, and outlying areas, one as far afield as the town of Barrie, fifty-six miles (ninety kilometers) north of the city. While many of these buildings are architecturally engaging, it is beyond the scope of this guidebook to include individual entries on them. A list of affiliated hospitals and centers is included below for those readers who want to explore one of North America's largest health-sciences constellations.

Hospitals and Centers Affiliated with the University of Toronto Health Sciences Programs:

Full Affiliates

Baycrest Centre for Geriatric Care, Bloorview Kids Rehab, Centre for Addiction and Mental Health, Hospital for Sick Children, Mount Sinai Hospital, St. Michael's Hospital, Sunnybrook Health Sciences Centre, Toronto Rehabilitation Institute, University Health Network (Toronto General Hospital, Princess Margaret Hospital, and Toronto Western Hospital), and Women's College Hospital

Community Affiliates

Bridgepoint Health, Credit Valley Hospital, George Hull Centre for Children and Families, Hincks-Dellcrest Centre, Humber River Regional Hospital, North York General Hospital, Providence Healthcare, Royal Victoria Hospital, Scarborough Hospital, St. John's Rehabilitation Hospital, St. Joseph's Health Centre, Surrey Place Centre, Toronto East General Hospital, Trillium Health Centre, and West Park Healthcare Centre

Medical Sciences Building

75. Medical Sciences Building

Govan Kaminker Langley Keenleyside Melick Devonshire & Wilson with Somerville McMurrich & Oxley, 1969

The seven-story Medical Sciences Building, known as "Med Sci," houses the Faculty of Medicine, founded in 1843. It is one of the largest, and strangest, buildings on campus, with a "shaggy-dog" precast concrete cladding that serves as a reminder of the hallucinatory, anything-goes late-1960s era it was built in.

Med Sci is composed of deep, solid blocks so that little natural light reaches the center of the building, reinforcing its highly internalized nature. Mazelike corridors with beige concrete-block walls make the interior seem like a cross between a no-nonsense high school and a low-cost hospital. In contrast, the exterior surfaces command attention. Project architect Peter Goering convinced the university to devote public art funds allocated for the building to the fabrication of an artful facade. Serving simultaneously as a rain-screen system (technically innovative at the time) and a grand sculpture project, the precast cladding's surface was designed by multidisciplinary artist Robert Downing, who, in association with his former sculpture professor, Ted Bieler, worked collaboratively with Beer Precast Concrete, Ltd. (In addition to his imaginative contribution to the building's surfaces, Downing executed two interior relief walls, and Bieler contributed both the *Wave* ground sculpture in the courtyard and the vertical *Helix of Life*, which stands near the main entrance.) Downing was interested in the intersection of modern technology and spirituality, and was also deeply focused on what he called "organic geometry." By the time he died in 1997, he had become a noted and notorious (for his early LSD-imbibing days) artist in Canada.

Med Sci's eccentrically ribbed coat lends it an air of surreality, made even more bizarre by the presence of a fine statue of Robert Raikes, founder of the Sunday School Movement in England in 1780, which stands at the building's northeast corner. On the north face of Med Sci, Downing's obsession with organic geometry comes into full bloom. Here, robust Virginia Creeper vines grow up six stories through the sculpted concrete, and cold abstraction and thriving greenery intertwine.

In 2005 Behnisch, Behnisch & Partner linked the Medical Sciences Building southward to the new Terrence Donnelly Centre for Cellular and Biomolecular Research with an attractive cafeteria. The architects cleverly captured a panel of Downing and Bieler's sculpted wall and integrated it into the east wall of the addition. This element and the shaggy walls beyond now seem curiously contemporary, showing how architectural tastes and criticism often come full circle. Indeed, it is not surprising that today's digitally savvy architecture students are fascinated by the building's sculpted relief patterns, which, forty years later, match their own preoccupations with complex surface manipulation.

76. Terrence Donnelly Centre for Cellular and Biomolecular Research (CCBR)

architectsAlliance and Behnisch, Behnisch & Partner, 2005

Terrence Donnelly Centre for Cellular and Biomolecular Research

The cutting-edge research that goes on within the Terrence Donnelly Centre for Cellular and Biomolecular Research (Donnelly CCBR) is as progressive as its design. The Donnelly CCBR, with its open, flexible, loftlike spaces, encourages interaction between the four hundred researchers from the fields of medicine, pharmacy, applied science and engineering, and arts and science that work there. The idea for this interdisciplinary research facility came from Dr. James Friesen and Dr. Cecil Yip, professors and colleagues in the Faculty of Medicine. (A plaque recognizing their contribution to the project is affixed to

Terrence Donnelly Centre for Cellular and Biomolecular Research

one of the ovoid seminar rooms on the main level.) In the late 1990s Friesen and
Yip collaborated with the university's Design Review Committee to launch an international search for an architect, resulting in the selection of the innovative Stuttgart-
based firm Behnisch, Behnisch & Partner, working closely with the Toronto firm
architectsAlliance. The center was named to recognize the generous financial support of retired lawyer and businessman Terrence Donnelly.

A constricted but interesting site became available for the Donnelly CCBR
when the university decided to close down Taddle Creek Road, which in the
nineteenth century ran northwest from College Street to University College but
in recent years only extended one block north of College Street. University planners and the architects decided to set the building 170 feet (50 meters) back from
College Street, thus generating a south-facing forecourt. The center was integrated
with the Medical Sciences Building to the north and with two heritage buildings
flanking the site: the Rosebrugh Building to the west and the FitzGerald Building
to the east. The east facade of the nearby Mining Building also added positively
to the emerging open space. Landscape architect Diana Gerrard composed the
forecourt as a series of energetic, sloping diagonals, rendered elegantly in black
granite, pink-gray granite, and stainless steel. A figurative sculpture titled *Spirit of
Discovery*, by Veronica and Edwin Dam de Nogales, stands in a grove of birch trees
at the west side of the forecourt.

LEFT: *CCBR sky garden and stair*
RIGHT: *FitzGerald Building*

Rising from this sunny, well-used public space, the elongated, transparent, twelve-story Donnelly CCBR embraces sustainable design principles. The tower of repetitive laboratory zones (recessed at the seventh floor to accommodate mechanical equipment and to scale the building down) has a double-skin facade on the south to help reduce heat loss and provide wind and acoustical modulation. This laboratory volume sits atop a public concourse that steps up to and connects with the Medical Sciences Building. A winter garden grows between the Donnelly CCBR and the Rosebrugh Building, and is complemented on upper levels of the tower with three south-facing interior "sky gardens" that adjoin faculty-student lounges. The building is particularly spectacular at night, when it is glowing in its colorful nakedness, and a sense of the synergistic scientific work on molecular genetics comes alive.

77. FitzGerald Building *Mathers & Haldenby, 1926*

This red brick building was constructed in the mid-1920s to house the School of Hygiene, which was dedicated to public health and preventive medicine. It was later named in honor of Dr. John Gerald FitzGerald, one of the fathers of the progressive provincial and federal health care programs that now exist in Canada. Currently, the FitzGerald Building contains various divisions of the Faculty of Medicine, such as anesthesia, cardiovascular sciences, radiation oncology, and medical imaging.

The FitzGerald Building originally faced Taddle Creek Road, later closed. Now, even in its somewhat demoted status in the shadows of the Donnelly CCBR and the Leslie L. Dan Pharmacy Building, it contributes significantly, along with the Mining and Rosebrugh buildings, to the shaping of the Donnelly CCBR forecourt. Though stylistically different, these buildings form a new ensemble that proves old and new can fit together successfully.

A mildly Georgian-style structure with an E-shaped footprint, the FitzGerald Building is typical of the low-key, conservative architecture of Mathers & Haldenby.

Tanz Neuroscience Building (right) and Leslie L. Dan Pharmacy Building (left)

Handsome stone carving, delicate glasswork, and bracketed lamps enliven the entrances. Inside, a fine lobby sports a marble floor, a handsome chandelier, and a wall inscription from the nineteenth-century English biologist and agnostic Thomas Henry Huxley, on the importance of a liberal education and a directive for individuals "to respect others as himself."

78. Tanz Neuroscience Building   *Mathers & Haldenby, 1931*

While designed by the same architects as the nearby FitzGerald Building, the Tanz Neuroscience Building is more architecturally ambitious. Originally the university's Botany Building, it had elegant greenhouses extending from its south face. (Completed in 1932, they were designed by Mathers & Haldenby in association with

Lord & Burnham, a company that specializes in greenhouse structures.) The greenhouses were removed in 2003/04 to make way for the new Leslie L. Dan Pharmacy Building, and major portions were reconstructed in Allan Gardens, a public park twelve blocks to the east, where they now serve as the Children's Conservatory.)

The stone-clad Tanz Building is handsomely proportioned and, with its angled front elevation facing Queen's Park, polite in urban disposition. It is a curious architectural hybrid: while it is generally Georgian-revival in style, it also incorporates modern steel-casement windows. Inside, the building is humble, featuring a petite octagonal lobby faced in Manitoba Tyndall stone and a floor of inlaid marble.

The respect commanded by the Tanz Building is evident in Foster + Partners' concept for the new Leslie L. Dan Pharmacy Building directly to the south. The firm admired the 1930s building, and drew and extended southward an imagined horizontal line at the height of the Tanz Building's parapet, which determined the height of the Pharmacy Building's grand lobby's ceiling and became the starting point for the laboratory "cube" above. The two buildings now sit comfortably side by side, sharing a pleasant courtyard between them. The building currently houses various medical divisions, including the Tanz Centre for Research in Neurodegenerative Diseases, created through a gift in 1987 from land developer Mark Tanz and his family.

79. Leslie L. Dan Pharmacy Building

Foster + Partners with Moffat Kinoshita Architects, Inc. (later Cannon Design), 2006

By 2000 the province of Ontario was facing a critical shortage of pharmacists. With this news, the University of Toronto Faculty of Pharmacy set out to double its enrollment and expand its research agenda. Leslie L. Dan, a 1954 graduate of the school, made a significant gift for an ambitious new facility that was named in his honor. "Tailor-made" seems an apt description for the building, because it both admirably fits its teaching agenda and has been crafted like a fine English suit by London-based Foster + Partners, the architects responsible for this restrained yet bold structure facing Queen's Park.

Its prominent site, edged on the north and west by historic buildings, already had a set of much-loved greenhouses dating from 1932 that presented challenging preservation issues. Technologically past their prime, the greenhouses were no longer useful to the university, and the most architecturally significant portions were relocated to the city's Allan Gardens.

Even with the greenhouses gone, a very small site was left for the 167,000-square-foot (16,500-square-meter) Pharmacy Building. Lord Foster and his

Leslie L. Dan Pharmacy Building

team devised a simple, three-volume scheme that maximizes use of the available land by placing two large lecture halls in an underground volume and setting a laboratory/office "glass cube" on slender concrete columns atop a transparent, five-story atrium. The architects cleverly aligned the bottom of the elevated, glass-clad cube with the cornices of the adjacent historic buildings. The Pharmacy Building's rationally knit-together spaces, profusion of natural light, and precise detailing create an impressive if somewhat cold atmosphere, made chillier by the ice-blue core walls.

Two wonderfully mysterious, ovoid forms float above a coffee shop and seating area in the grand lobby. These pods, which seem to defy gravity, were constructed as "steel baskets" and suspended by steel rods. They contain seminar rooms and have student and faculty lounges carved into their tops. At night, computer-programmed lighting bounces off the pods and the lobby's soaring glass walls, presenting a theatrical display for passersby.

The Leslie L. Dan Pharmacy Building's generosity of scale and overall aesthetic clarity enable it to play a significant role at the junction of University Avenue and College Street. Its stately concrete columns and elegant, fritted-glass cladding relate well to the materials employed in the Ontario Hydro Building to the south. With the completion in 2010 of the twenty-three-story, glass-clad west tower of the MaRS Centre diagonally opposite, the Pharmacy Building will participate in an even grander urban composition at this key Toronto intersection.

80. Health Sciences Building *Page & Steele Architects, 1961*
Renovations *Stantec Architecture, 2006*

A decade ago, with few sites available for new construction and open space becoming more desirable on the St. George campus, the University of Toronto began to acquire major buildings around its periphery for future teaching and research purposes. When the Education Centre at the southeast corner of College and McCaul streets became available in 2003, the university purchased the 200,000-square-foot (18,580-square-meter) structure.

Renovated and renamed the Health Sciences Building, it now houses the Lawrence S. Bloomberg Faculty of Nursing and an array of departments from the Faculty of Medicine, including the Dala Lana School of Public Health. The facility promotes collaboration with many of the university's affiliated teaching hospitals and research institutes.

Designed for the Toronto Board of Education by the prominent Toronto firm Page & Steele Architects, the eight-story Education Centre was a strong example of mid-century modernism that provided a comfortable environment for innovative research and training in education.

LEFT: *Health Sciences Building*
RIGHT: *263 McCaul Street*

The building's concrete structure is clad in Indiana limestone and Deer Island gray granite from Georgia; the main entrance is surfaced in mirror-finished stainless steel; and the suave two-story foyer sports Loredo Chiaro marble walls and a travertine floor. But there is much more to celebrate here than the handsome 1960s material palette. The north and south facades, which, in their rhythmic fenestration patterns are reminiscent of piano keyboards, richly engage light and shadow. A mechanical penthouse enclosed in translucent glass glides coolly above these sculpted faces. Glazed in metal sashes with fixed, cast-wire glass between precast concrete fins, the penthouse is among the most attractive in Toronto.

The original Education Centre included a number of distinctive interior murals created by Stefan Fritz and Merton Chambers, and a lovely exterior relief by Elizabeth Hahn—an ambitious program of art intended to express the ideals and prominence of the city's educational system. Fortunately, the university preserved these spirited works in the new spaces of the Health Sciences Building.

81. 263 McCaul Street *Charles H. Bishop, 1916*

Among the university's hidden architectural gems is the original Toronto Board of Education Administration Building, a grand beaux arts edifice designed by Charles H. Bishop, who served as architect for the board of education from 1888 until 1919 and is credited with the design of more than fifty schools in the Toronto area, many of which still stand today.

The building fronted on College Street until 1959, when it was moved south to make way for the new Education Centre. Now the old Board of Education building is a kind of lonely island—hard to find and difficult to access—and its original grand entrance sits high above a service ramp, absent its front steps. The building's old address plate, "155," still hangs next to the front door, along with original plaques that announce the board's now nonexistent office hours. Above the old entrance, a magnificent porch and window composition is marked by Ionic columns.

Today, 263 McCaul houses the Department of Family and Community Medicine, Environmental Health and Safety, and other divisions, but there are still remnants of its time serving the board of education. The handsome west stairwell contains wonderful pictures of chairmen and public officials of the Toronto Public School Board from the mid-nineteenth century onward, and the Toronto District School Board Sesquicentennial Museum and Archives is tucked away in the building, almost unnoticed.

82. Examination Facility *Cyril E. Dyson, 1931*
Renovations *Montgomery Sisam Architects, 2008*

Examination Facility

This large building was constructed for the Toronto Board of Education as a supply facility and depot for the repair and refurbishing of school equipment. Cyril E. Dyson, who served as architect for the board from 1921 to 1950, designed the center in a mildly art deco style, and it was purchased by the university in 2002.

Basically a utilitarian warehouse structure built close to the street, the building does have some surprising ornamental touches, evident on the doorways on the 255 McCaul Street facade and on the south-facing doorways at 20 and 22 Orde Street, which offer pairs of fruit-filled urns cast in stone. The east, south, and west elevations of the center have vertical brick piers, between which hang new energy-efficient windows sympathetic in scale and style to the industrial, steel-framed windows that they replaced. On the west face, a slender brick pier magically morphs into a minitower at the main entrance, marked at just the right moment by a circular window.

The university recently renovated the building to create a new testing center, the largest of its kind in North America, that will also serve as a study hub and special events facility. The renovations include a handsome new entrance and lobby and provide a range of rooms for mid-semester and final examinations.

LEFT: *Banting Institute*
RIGHT: *Best Institute*

83. Banting Institute *Darling & Pearson, 1930*

The Banting Institute is named for Sir Frederick Banting, the Nobel Prize–winning Toronto surgeon and scientist who successfully developed insulin with Dr. Charles H. Best in the laboratory of Dr. J. J. R. Macleod between 1920 and 1922. (The 1923 Nobel Prize in Medicine was shared between Banting and Macleod.) Until late 2008 the building hosted various medical departments.

Symmetrically composed and clad in red brick, the Banting Institute faces College Street with a handsome front entrance, leading to an attractive foyer featuring a portrait of Banting. Considering that the building was designed by the famed Toronto firm Darling & Pearson, its architecture seems rather matter-of-fact. This could be because the firm's leading light, Frank Darling, died in 1923, and architects with less talent took over. Whatever the reasons for its underdeveloped design, the building continues, eighty years later, to serve as a useful "swing facility" for a broad range of university uses.

84. Best Institute *Mathers & Haldenby, 1954*

Directly west of the Banting Institute sits the Best Institute, an appropriate pairing considering that Dr. Charles H. Best, the building's namesake, worked together with Sir Frederick Banting to develop insulin in the 1920s. Architects Mathers & Haldenby oriented the Best Insitute's principal, symmetrical facade westward,

Joint Centre for Bioethics

toward the grand mall of Queen's Park. While the front lawn of the Best Institute remains, the building's formal relationship to Queen's Park has slowly eroded, first compromised by the 1964 Frost (South) Building at 7 Queen's Park Crescent East, then compromised further by the recent construction of the Ontario Fire Fighter Memorial in front of the institute.

A portrait of Best by the noted artist Cleeve Horne graces the front lobby, and nearby hangs a small landscape painting by Best, who was also an amateur artist. At the center of the lobby an intriguing scientific instrument is on display: the colorimeter used by Banting and Best in their development of insulin.

85. Joint Centre for Bioethics *Smith & Gemmell, 1883*

Originally built as the Zion Congregational Church by Smith & Gemmell, the architects who designed the original Knox College and the Church of the Redeemer at the northeast corner of Bloor Street West and Avenue Road, the building's steep, slate-tiled roof, Gothic-style windows, and sturdily crafted doorways speak of the faith and hope of two centuries ago. The university acquired the building in 1965.

Offices and meeting rooms have been awkwardly shoehorned into the former church to house the Joint Centre for Bioethics, but the soaring central space still exists, and among the makeshift partitions one can still glimpse the patterned brick walls, lovely wood beams and brackets supporting the roof, and colorful stained-glass windows. This former place of worship still retains many traces of history and deserves sympathetic renovation and renewal.

MaRS Centre

86. MaRS Centre *Darling & Pearson, 1912*
East tower, south tower, and renovations *Adamson Associates Architects, 2005*
West tower *Bregman + Hamann, 2010*

Located on College Street directly across from the university's Banting and Best institutes and adjacent to Toronto General Hospital, MaRS is an innovation center engaged in a broad spectrum of research, including biotechnology, advanced information technology, and nanotechnology. Founded in 2000 and funded by government, industry, and private initiatives, the MaRS Centre is not part of the university but is strongly affiliated with it. The architecturally ambitious MaRS complex

MaRS Centre, rendering of west tower

consists of the historic Toronto General Hospital building—its central set piece—and three sleek new additions, including "bookend" tower blocks to the east and west of the hospital building. When the phase two west tower is completed in 2010, MaRS will have 1.5 million square feet (13,935 square meters) of interior floor space.

The histories of the center's site and the former hospital are fascinating. The Toronto General Hospital complex originally consisted of eleven buildings spread over nine acres with landscaped gardens and lawns at its center, and at one point it was the largest private hospital in North America. It was also considered one of the most modern hospitals in the world and for decades was the site of collaborative research with the university, spawning such medical breakthroughs as the artificial kidney and the pacemaker. The iconic central portion facing College Street, designed by Darling & Pearson in an eclectic Renaissance style, contained the hospital's administration building, which was flanked on one side by the surgical wing and on the other by the medical wing.

Thankfully, the magnificent 1912 Administration Building and the wings facing College Street were preserved, revitalized, and integrated into the new MaRS complex. Its beautifully proportioned domed cupola rising above the central entrance was lovingly restored, as were the terra-cotta and Roman-length brick (ranging in color from flecked-golden to deep bronze-purple) facade materials. The rear south end of the former hospital faces a long east-west atrium that connects the bookend towers. The metallic Toronto Medical Discovery Tower to the east, completed in 2005, defers to the central heritage building, while the twenty-three-story west tower (currently under construction) is somewhat more ambitious architecturally. It will have a four-story glass cube (christened "the jewel box") at its northwest corner, diagonally across from the glass-clad cubic forms of the university's Foster

+ Partners–designed Leslie L. Dan Pharmacy Building. The new tower will have a direct connection into the Queen's Park subway station. MaRS's front lawn along College Street draws inspiration from the hospital's original landscape plan and includes portions of the beautiful iron fence that once ran the full length of the block.

87. Dentistry Building *Allward & Gouinlock Architects, 1959*
Addition *Allward & Gouinlock Architects, 1985*

Dentistry Building

The School of Dentistry (now the Faculty of Dentistry) is located near the many teaching hospitals that stretch along University Avenue. Founded by the Royal College of Dental Surgeons of Ontario in 1875, it became affiliated with the University of Toronto in 1888. Visitors arriving in the south lobby of Canada's largest dental school are greeted by a huge colorful, but rather unsettling, mural on the subject of pain, executed in 1978 by artist Carmen Cereceda.

As completed in 1959, the buff brick International Style building had 183,000 square feet (17,000 square meters) of floor space. Originally U-shaped, with a dominant five-story wing along the south and lower three-story wings on the east and north, the building's courtyard was filled in with a major addition at the north and west sides in 1985. Inside the Faculty of Dentistry, a vast two-story clinic on the east side of the second floor is filled with a sea of dental examination chairs. A long horizontal band of windows flood the room with natural light. Also on the second floor is the jam-packed and extremely interesting Dental Museum, founded by the Royal College of Dental Surgeons of Ontario in 1869.

WALK SEVEN: UNIVERSITY OF TORONTO
SCARBOROUGH (UTS)

MORNINGSIDE AVE

ELLESMERE ROAD

MILITARY TRAIL

Walk Seven: University of Toronto Scarborough (UTS)

Located twenty miles (thirty-two kilometers) east of the university's downtown St. George campus, the University of Toronto Scarborough (UTS) was established in 1964 as Scarborough College, beginning with evening classes held in a local high school. The first building, designed by architect John Andrews, opened in January 1966. Today UTS boasts more than ten thousand students enrolled in almost 200 undergraduate and graduate programs. As the juxtaposition of on-campus housing for about 760 students and more than three thousand parking spaces reveals, it is largely a commuter campus. However, "car culture" does not entirely dominate, and students enjoy an increasingly pedestrian-friendly three hundred-acre campus in one of Toronto's most dramatic natural landscapes, the Highland Creek Valley.

The sprawling suburban area known as Scarborough comprises more than 600,000 people and was a separate municipality until 1998, when it was amalgamated into the City of Toronto. Elizabeth Simcoe, wife of the first lieutenant governor of Upper Canada, Sir John Graves Simcoe, chose the name Scarborough for the precinct in the eighteenth century, because the geological features along Lake Ontario reminded her of the limestone cliffs in Scarborough, England.

It was surely both the raw power of the Highland Creek Valley landscape and the reality of the cold north that inspired architect John Andrews to sculpt his bold, megastructural vision of Scarborough College. Australian-born Andrews had been a finalist in the 1958 international design competition for Toronto City Hall and, although Viljo Revell's scheme was selected instead of his, he stayed in Toronto to work with the firm of John B. Parkin Associates, the local architects for the new city hall. During the early 1960s, when he was working on Scarborough College, Andrews was a professor of architecture at the University of Toronto. Together with colleagues Michael Hugo-Brunt (planner) and Michael Hough (landscape

Aerial view of Scarborough College, September 1966; Science Wing (left) and Humanities Wing (right)

architect), he developed a master plan for the new college in six weeks. The design was influenced by William Beckel, a young professor in the Department of Zoology who conducted pedagogical experiments using closed-circuit television at the university's main St. George campus. Scarborough was conceived in part as a "TV College," and each classroom was connected to a central TV production facility.

Andrews and his team designed a linear, concrete building with a stepped, pyramidal cross section and a system of internal pedestrian streets as the connective tissue. The first buildings of Scarborough College—the humanities and science wings—were completed in late 1965, and the astonishing project became an international destination for architecture students and architects. Although not universally loved, Andrews's high-image design branded Scarborough College, and the institution continues to wrestle with this, at times enthusiastically respecting and extending Andrews's legacy while at other times giving only lip service to it.

The fact remains that Scarborough College is one of Canada's most important modern buildings, and it propelled Andrews into national and international spotlights. Indeed, it can easily be argued that Scarborough College, along with Moshe Safdie's Habitat for Expo 67 in Montreal, is one of the two iconic works of twentieth-century Canadian architecture that continue to resonate internationally.

Enrollment on the Scarborough campus grew rapidly during the 1990s, reaching a population of five thousand students, and in 2000, the university commissioned the Toronto firm of Baird Sampson Neuert to develop a comprehensive master plan for future expansion. Barry Sampson of Baird Sampson Neuert revealed a deep understanding of Andrews's organic principles of flexibility and growth, while also accepting the realities of several unsympathetic additions that had been inflicted on the campus over the three decades since the original Andrews buildings. An intelligent new master plan resulted, which has generally been followed during the past five years of rapid expansion, although with mixed results architecturally. The increased densification and attention to landscape are admirable; however, one might question the overly diverse palette of materials and colors—charcoal brick, orange-tan brick, yellow brick, copper, green-glass curtain wall, among many others—which undermines visual coherence. Moreover, many of the recent buildings sit "on the earth" rather than being embedded in and seeming to grow from it, as Andrews's original buildings do so convincingly.

88. Humanities and Science Wings
John Andrews Architects with Page & Steele Architects; Michael Hough, landscape architect, 1966

Conceived as part of a larger, megastructural master plan for Scarborough College, the two wings were built in just over twenty-four months starting in 1963 and opened in January 1966. The Science Wing runs east-west along the ridge of the Highland Creek Valley, with the Humanities Wing running north-south. The two connect at an "elbow" consisting of a four-story central meeting place and a large outdoor patio, providing a framed view of the valley and river below. Tucked into the hillside, the wings vary from five to six stories, and the complex is connected by a linear pedestrian street that protects against winter harshness and, like a small village, encourages socializing.

John Andrews was the driving force behind the willful design, but the role of Michael Hough, the university's campus landscape architect at the time, was significant. Hough started analyzing the site before Andrews became fully engaged, and he brought a progressive environmental perspective to the project. Hough maintained that the new buildings should protect the existing slope and prevent erosion, and he brought in climatologists and other experts to ensure an environmental approach. Then-president Claude Bissel also fully endorsed the environmental emphasis.

Andrews's forms are highly sculptural and masterful in their composition. The long horizontals are marked near the center elbow by the vertical thrust of the power plant chimneys (see page 198), reminiscent of Italian Futurist architect Antonio Sant'Elia's visionary Citta Nuova project of 1914. Just as the Futurists embraced the industrial world and emphasized audacity and energy, so did Andrews half a century later. Together, the Humanities and Science wings read as a giant educational machine charging through the landscape, spinning out knowledge. Like Sant'Elia, Andrews loved the brute authority of "industrial" reinforced concrete, and there is little escape from it in his design, both inside and outside. Thankfully, the floors of the internal street and the collective spaces are paved in terra-cotta-color English quarry tile. These handsome floors, fine-scaled vertical wood paneling, and abundant natural light flowing from skylights humanize the great machine.

In its composition and treatment of volume, Andrews's work at Scarborough is ambitious, to say the least. The pyramidal stepped forms respond locally to program, with classrooms, laboratories, auditoria, offices, and stairs given strong sculptural expression. The west-facing side of the Humanities Wing presents an array of stacked auditoria with sloping walls that look almost Mayan (see page 31), while the south facade of the Science Wing is arranged in descending terraces knit together by two monumental sloping service ducts. To the university's credit, it has preserved these important mid-twentieth-century buildings and, when changes became necessary, made modifications with care, a recent example being the elegant glass mechanical penthouse enclosure designed by Jon Neuert of Baird Sampson Neuert Architects.

Architect Andrews once claimed that "only architecture that meets the needs of people endures." In his understanding these needs comprised, on the one hand,

Science Wing, Central Meeting Place

notions of monumentality and energy and, on the other, a range of rather everyday human activities such as casual street encounters. Andrews gave Scarborough a brilliantly inspiring and enduring work of architecture. At the same time, and somewhat ironically, the buildings' "mega" quality and the insistent gray roughness of the exposed concrete have not met certain psychological needs; this has caused the university to aspire in recent years to smaller-scaled, gentler, less mechanistic designs for new construction on the Scarborough campus.

Although some of the new buildings are quite successful, it is regrettable that Andrews's clear vision has been so compromised. Walking along the ravine side of the Humanities Wing, one encounters a sculpture titled *A Tall Couple*, by Louis Archambault, originally commissioned for Expo 67 in Montreal, then donated to Scarborough College by the House of Seagram. Pausing near this fine sculpture, with Andrews's structure rising above and the landscape rolling dramatically down to the river below, it is hard to deny the enduring spiritual presence of this remarkable building.

89. Bladen Wing (R-Wing)
John Andrews International Pty. Ltd, 1973

Bladen Wing (left), chimneys at Humanities Wing (right)

Seven years after Andrews's Humanities and Science wings opened and in accordance with his master plan, a third wing was added to the northeast on essentially flat land. Originally known as the R-Wing, it incorporated classrooms, office space, a gymnasium, and other sports facilities. In 1982 the east side of the R-Wing was extended with the Vincent W. Bladen Library, named in memory of a former member of Scarborough's economics department. (The Bladen Library was absorbed into the new Academic Resource Centre in 2003.)

With the addition of the new wing in 1973, Andrews's composition became Y-shaped, extending the original ridge buildings to the campus's entrance on Military Trail. The R-Wing connected to the Humanities Wing under the podium level and via an enclosed bridge at the second floor, adjacent to the power plant chimneys. The bridge created a framed view and a strong east-west visual corridor. In 2003, with the visual axis to the east greatly strengthened

Academic Resource Centre

by the construction of Joan Foley Hall, the Academic Learning Centre, and the Management Building, the overhead bridge was removed. Traces of it remain on the west side of the power plant.

Although its location religiously followed Andrews's master plan, the R-Wing had little of the conceptual, spatial, and material rigor of the original buildings. Drastic budget reductions during design and the fact that, by the early 1970s, Andrews was less focused on Toronto and had started establishing a practice in his native Australia dragged the project down, with the result that it feels more like a suburban high school than a dignified place of higher learning.

With the addition of the Academic Resource Centre to the east in 2003 and the completion of the Arts and Administration Building to the west in 2005—the latter generating a lovely narrow courtyard—the Bladen Wing is now luckily pretty much buried at the center of campus.

90. Academic Resource Centre (ARC)
Brian MacKay-Lyons in association with Rounthwaite, Dick and Hadley Architects, Inc., 2003

Designed by Halifax-based architect and urban designer Brian MacKay-Lyons, the low-slung, Academic Resource Centre (ARC) includes the renovated Vincent W. Bladen Library, the Sun Microsystems Informatics Commons, the Doris McCarthy Gallery, and a five hundred-seat lecture theater. It merges with the 1973 R-Wing and contributes significantly to the formation of the east-west pedestrian walkway

walkway that runs from the heart of the campus east to Joan Foley Hall and the South Residences.

MacKay-Lyons used a tartan grid as the basic ordering device for the ARC, both for space planning and the building structure. It is akin to Louis Kahn's concept of "served and servant" spaces, wherein circulation and support systems are relegated to secondary zones, freeing up large, flexible areas in between. The architect applied this system rigorously in the ARC, extending linear strips of the tartan south, beyond the building, to generate an elegant courtyard. Viewed against the horizontal copper cladding that has turned an inviting chocolate-brown color, the white birch trees populating the courtyard are a lovely sight.

Besides the spatial geometry of the tartan grid, the ARC's interior displays an intentionally frugal material vocabulary of concrete floors and unpainted concrete block, warmed with wood furnishings and fittings. MacKay-Lyons's architecture consistently shows conceptual clarity and economy of means, but here the architect also made a concerted effort to link to the boldness and toughness of Andrews's legacy. The Academic Learning Centre has a strong, organic sense of place. Simply stated, it fits.

91. Student Centre *Stantec Architecture Ltd., 2004*

Entering the Scarborough campus at the main entrance on Military Trail, one is struck by the dramatic structural cantilever and the soaring butterfly roof of the Student Centre. This three-story, 48,000-square-foot (4,460 square meters) building houses offices of student organizations and student affairs, the health center, the equity office, a food court, a restaurant/pub, a multifaith chapel, the campus radio station, a games room, study areas, and retail stores. It is uncompromisingly modern—overtly optimistic, ready to fly.

A lot of spatial and topographical maneuvering was required for the tight site, which had to absorb the campus's main shipping and receiving ramp leading underground along the center's east edge. A lawn slopes down to a basement-level pub and outdoor deck at the northwest corner. To the south, the Student Centre reaches out toward the Arts and Administration Building with two wings. If somewhat erratic in composition and material palette, the architectural gymnastics do contribute to the building's social liveliness. Visually, there seems to be something for everyone. Indeed, the building has become the gateway to the campus and a real hub of student activity.

Environmental sustainability played an important role in the design, and the architects worked closely with the student stakeholders to explore innovative techniques to minimize environmental consequences through efficient use of energy and resources. The building was imaginatively designed to reduce energy

Student Centre

consumption, and eighteen tons of steel were reused from demolition at the Royal Ontario Museum. The project achieved silver status within the LEED program (Leadership in Energy and Environmental Design) and received a 2005 Green Design award from the city of Toronto.

92. Arts and Administration Building
Montgomery Sisam Architects, 2005

The most recent of the three new buildings constructed at the core of the Scarborough campus is the unassuming yet substantial Arts and Administration Building. Situated behind the Student Centre and thoughtfully linked to it by an elegant pergola along the east side, the yellow-brick Arts and Administration Building is angled on the west to form a kind of prow. This prow, which faces the main entrance driveway into the campus with a huge double-height window, signals one of the building's roles, which is to serve as a visitor's center. For most newcomers to the campus, the Arts and Administration Building is the point of orientation and welcoming.

And this role it serves well. Within a plan configuration and systems of detailing that seem partly inspired by the original Andrews-designed buildings and partly derived from Montgomery and Sisam's long-standing interest in the work of Finnish architect Alvar Aalto, there is a sense of flow, comfort, and ease. At the south end of the building, located at the very heart of campus, is a handsomely designed volume containing the institution's seat of governance, the Council Chamber. This is a

TOP: *Arts and Administration Building*
BOTTOM: *Science Building*

Courtyard, Arts and Administration Building

tall, grand room with vertical wood-slot paneling, generous amounts of natural light, and brown leather chairs. If the former Andrews-designed Council Chamber in the Humanities Wing was quirky in its castlelike extreme, the new Council Chamber is the opposite: calm and dignified.

The slender courtyard formed between the Arts and Administration Building and the Bladen Wing, designed by Janet Rosenburg Associates, represents landscape architecture at its best, with subtly angled walkways, gracious and varied plant material, and pleasant night lighting making this little place a gem.

93. Science Building *Moriyama & Teshima Architects, 2008*

The new Science Building is connected to the northwest end of Andrews's 1966 Science Wing. The facility houses sixteen laboratories, offices for faculty and research assistants, and a 235-seat lecture theater. Resulting in part from strong prodding from the university's Design Review Committee, the location, footprint, and materials of the new Science Building are sympathetic with and extend Andrews's original megastructure. With its generosity of scale, long bands of horizontal windows, and charcoal-color zinc cladding, the building makes a positive impression in the landscape when viewed from a distance. Sweeping to the north, it also contributes to the positive shaping of an emerging grand west lawn. Unlike the Management Building, which remains physically unconnected to the Humanities Wing and thus seems adrift, the Science Building reads as a familial architectural extension and, hopefully, signals a recommitment to Andrews's vision.

Management Building

94. Management Building
Kuwabara Payne McKenna Blumberg Architects, 2004

Similar to other recently constructed buildings on the Scarborough campus, the Management Building was done on a modest budget that makes the Andrews heydays seem very distant. The masonry and glass curtain-wall structure has a slightly cranked plan that inflects toward and attempts to relate to the nearby Humanities Wing. However, the exterior barely resonates with Andrews's building, and only inside is there a sense of connection to the spirit of the 1960s megastructure. The primary interior move is a spatially exhilarating, four-story atrium that provides a communal focus for students. Natural light flows down through the space, enlivening the concrete structure, charcoal-color masonry block walls, polished concrete floor, and cherry paneling. A dignified multipurpose room opens southward to an outdoor courtyard, and from here one can enjoy the insistent horizontals of the elegant south elevation, which is the most successful face of the building.

Management's front door faces onto the east-west pedestrian spine of the campus, and there is an attempt to anchor the building along this spine with a grand stair tower. Unfortunately, this undistinguished tower, clad in charcoal-color masonry units, competes uncomfortably with the glass-enclosed, axial tower of Joan Foley Hall further to the east.

Joan Foley Hall

The promise of the Management Building is that, someday, an infill structure will link it to the west with the Humanities Wing, thereby allowing the lovely atrium to be understood as not just an entity in itself but, rather, as a continuation of the Andrews-designed pedestrian street system.

95. Joan Foley Hall
Baird Sampson Neuert and Montgomery Sisam Architects, 2003

This 231-bed, apartment-style student residence was named in honor of the first female provost at the University of Toronto (and Scarborough's first female principal), Joan E. Foley, who began her teaching career in psychology in 1963. Since 1993 the university has presented the annual Joan E. Foley Quality of Student Experience Award to a student, faculty, or staff member.

The four-story structure rambles along the crest of the ravine and includes a sculptural, glazed tower, which visually anchors the eastern termination of the campus's east-west pedestrian spine. Clad in orange-tan brick and generous amounts of glass, Joan Foley Hall is exuberant in plan configuration while expressing simplicity in elevation. A bold and well-composed mechanical penthouse atop the southern wing is worth noting. Clustered apartments are cleverly distributed to maximize natural light from corner windows. Environmental responsibility and sustainability played an important role in the design, and the building is energy efficient.

Joan Foley Hall

On a campus that is dominated by commuting students, Joan Foley Hall is a welcome example of the kind of pleasant residential life that is possible at Scarborough.

96. N'sheemaehn Child Care Centre
Michael H. K. Wong Architects Inc., 1990

N'sheemaehn Child Care Centre

Conveniently located near the campus's main entrance, the economically designed N'sheemaehn Child Care Centre was built to serve both the local community and the university. Servicing and storage spaces wrap around a central open-plan hub. The center's indoor spaces are thoughtfully linked to generous outdoor play areas, the whole being nestled in the wooded surroundings.

97. Miller Lash House and Coach House
Attributed to Edward B. Green, Sr., 1913

At the southern edge of the Scarborough campus is the stately Miller Lash House, which serves as a conference center, guest house, and community events facility. Completed between 1911 and 1913 by Toronto businessman Miller Lash, whose father owned the Brazilian Traction, Light and Power Company Ltd., the seventeen-room house was the set piece of his family's 375-acre summer estate in the Highland Creek Valley.

Legend has it that in 1911 the wealthy Mr. Lash was out for a Sunday drive along what is now Old Kingston Road, which descends into the valley of Highland Creek. Lash was supposedly so impressed by the land with its grassy fields, forest, and rushing stream that he promptly bought the property and commissioned architect Edward B. Green, Sr., of the prominent Buffalo firm Green & Wicks to design his new estate.

The design of the Miller Lash House generally follows the style of the arts and crafts movement. The walls of the house are constructed of poured-in-place concrete and integrally faced with river stone collected from the Highland Creek bed, which meanders by the house. The heavy beams and trusswork that support the cathedral ceilings are squared pine timbers, while natural clay was used for the roof and floor tiles.

Miller Lash died in 1941, and the house was sold to insurance broker E. L. McLean, who, in 1963, sold the estate to the University of Toronto. The university renovated the house to serve as the principal's residence, in conjunction with the establishment of Scarborough College in 1964. A. F. Wynne Plumptre, appointed as the college's second principal, was the first principal to reside in the house. Principals continued to live there until 1976.

In 1998 the Miller Lash Estate was designated under the Ontario Heritage Act, and the university decided to restore the house. Through the determination and hard work of Lynn Dellandrea, the wife of UTS alumnus and University of Toronto vice-president Jon Dellandrea, Shane Baghai, a Toronto developer, and numerous volunteers, the unique house was lovingly restored, and efforts continue to acquire appropriate furnishings and complete the surrounding grounds.

98. Centennial HP Science and Technology Centre
Kuwabara Payne McKenna Blumberg Architects/Stone McQuire Vogt Architects, 2004

Although not administratively part of UTS, the Centennial HP [Hewlett Packard] Science and Technology Centre sits on land owned by the university, and the two institutions share several joint-degree programs, such as paramedicine, journalism, new media, environmental science, and industrial microbiology. Centennial College was established in 1966 as Ontario's first community college and now has four campuses and six satellite locations. It is recognized as one of the most culturally diverse post-secondary institutions in Canada with nearly one hundred ethnocultural groups represented and eighty languages spoken.

The V-shaped Centennial facility is reminiscent of a magnificent ocean liner that has somehow plowed into and comfortably come to rest in a south-facing hillside. Gleaming white in some places and metallic in others, this is undeniably optimistic architecture embodying a liberating spirit. Inside it feels like a small, bustling city with students coming and going amidst the central atrium commons space, classrooms, laboratories, exercise rooms, and a multifaith prayer room. Wandering through the Centennial HP Science and Technology Centre, one is reminded of Canada's aspirations as a microcosm of tolerance and social well-being, for which this humming place can serve as a rewarding everyday example.

Within this great "ship," a dramatic, four-story commons space steps down the hillside on several levels, flooded on the south by sunlight. A wood-clad lecture theater and classroom volume hovers above. This space has a convincing grandeur and sophistication while, at the same time, feeling relaxed and welcoming. Moreover, it has truly become the flagship building of the Centennial College system.

TOP: *Miller Lash House*

BOTTOM: *Centennial HP Science and Technology Centre*

WALK EIGHT: UNIVERSITY OF TORONTO MISSISSAUGA (UTM)

110

OUTER CIRCLE

OUTER CIRCLE

106

104

108

102

111

107

105

109

101

INNER CIRCLE

100

103

MISSISSAUGA ROAD

99

Walk Eight: University of Toronto Mississauga (UTM)

In 1963 the University of Toronto Plateau Committee recommended the establishment of two off-campus colleges: Scarborough College to the east of Toronto and Erindale College to the west. Erindale College, located twenty miles (thirty-three kilometers) west of downtown, along the Credit River, held its first classes in 1965 in the T. L. Kennedy Secondary School. The first class of ninety students graduated in 1970. Known since 1998 as the University of Toronto at Mississauga and more recently as simply University of Toronto Mississauga (UTM), the institution now has nearly eleven thousand students, 87 percent of them commuters.

The physical shape of the campus retains the traces of numerous master plans. In the thirty-five-year period from 1965 to 2000, UTM generated five different plans, resulting in the campus collage of divergent impulses that now exists. This history of moving in one direction for several years and then shifting to another has left behind superimposed, half-filled visions. Although the university's other suburban campus, at Scarborough (Walk Seven), has also seen erratic planning in recent decades, it at least has John Andrews's distinctive original buildings as a reminder of what a coherent campus plan might be.

UTM has not had the good fortune of Scarborough's Andrews legacy, but it almost did. In December 1966 the architect drafted an impressive thirty-one-page document titled "Erindale Campus Master Plan"—a bold, comprehensive proposal for consolidated, dense built form at the south end of the 224-acre campus and environmentally conscious conservation of the rest of the site. In terms of land use, it was a progressive proposition. Andrews had just completed his visionary project for the Scarborough campus, and the May 1966 "Report of the User's Committee on the Construction of the Erindale Campus, University of Toronto" stated, "We have been strongly impressed by the excellence of the Scarborough design, and have endeavored to profit from that example." It is thus not surprising that Andrews was called on again.

For Erindale, the architect's innovative team included planner Donovan Pinker, landscape architect Michael Hough, and housing consultant Evan Walker. Their proposal has several similarities with Scarborough: respect for and response to topography, separation of pedestrian and vehicular traffic, a climate-controlled pedestrian street system, integration of resident and commuter students, avoidance of rigid departmental structures, a strong emphasis on meeting and communal spaces, the use of television as a teaching aid, experimentation with modular building systems, and throughout, an elaborate orchestration of architectural space, as evident in the cross-section drawings drafted by the Andrews team.

The master plan gave special attention to commuting students. Andrews asserted that

Dr. Carl Williams, Vice-President for Planning for the Suburban Campuses and Principal, Erindale college (left) with William Davis, Premier of Ontario, at sod turning, Erindale College, 1966

the major innovation at Erindale will be the inclusion of a significant amount of 'bunk and carrel [*sic*]' space within the residential complex. This will mean that commuting students will be able to rent a bunk and carrell for overnight use whenever they wish to stay late on campus to work, or for some specific event....In this way it is hoped that commuters will become 2 or 3 day commuter residents, able to join more easily in the total student life of the university.

Andrews's vision was rigorously knit together in a proposed megastructure that grabbed the upper ridge of a former quarry and stepped down its slope. This building would be surrounded by carefully planned athletic fields, botanical gardens, research fields, and meadowlands (along with two thousand five hundred car spaces in four enclosed parking quays). The rollout of the plan was to happen incrementally, starting with five hundred students and growing to five thousand. Andrews prophetically imagined that eventually Erindale College would become a "town" of ten to twelve thousand students. The model prepared by Andrews's team gives a sense of the project's orthogonal, labyrinthine conception.

For reasons that remain unclear, however, within a year of the planning committee's recommendation the Andrews team was out of the picture, replaced by

Erindale College, perspective view, A. D. Margison & Associates Limited, 1968

A. D. Margison & Associates with Raymond Moriyama as planning and architectural consultant and J. Austin Floyd as landscape architect. Through late 1967 and early 1968, Moriyama developed a similarly ambitious megastructure, to be sited in exactly the same location that Andrews had selected, along the ridge of the quarry. Megastructural projects were *de rigueur* through the late 1950s and early 1960s, and both Andrews and Moriyama were undoubtedly influenced by European projects built during this period by architects such as Alison and Peter Smithson, Jacob B. Bakema, and Shadrach Woods. Many aspects of the officially adopted Margison-Moriyama plan were akin to Andrews's 1966 plan, such as the loop road, the separation of pedestrians from vehicles, the internal pedestrian street system, and the residence wings overlooking the river valley. It was a monumental conception that encompassed more than one million square feet.

Although the working relationship between Moriyama and the Margison firm from 1967 to 1968 is difficult to discern precisely, documentation from the period clearly reveals that Moriyama was involved in the Erindale project at key junctures. The forms that evolved during Moriyama's involvement were not as rigid as Andrews's and presented a somewhat more relaxed, organic approach. Indeed, the first part of the imagined megastructural colossus constructed at UTM—the Phase One Research and Laboratory Block, designed by Moriyama from 1967 to 1968 and opened in 1971—convincingly cranks and bends across the site (see pages 32 and 217). A. D. Margison & Associates designed the second phase—the 1973 Library, Lecture, Theatre Complex—which resembles Moriyama's first phase but lacks that design's material richness and formal finesse. Only these two phases of the Margison-Moriyama megastructure, which came to be known as the South Building, were realized.

By 1972 the Queen's Park government thought Ontario had excessive college and university capacity and put a halt to expansion. This, along with growing public and institutional skepticism of introverted, grandiose projects, put an end to UTM's imposing vision. By the 1970s and 1980s, funding was scarce and architectural ambition low. During that time, five architecturally undistinguished, entirely suburban town-house complexes for students were built around the campus, far removed both conceptually and physically from the original megastructure vision. By 2000, when Sterling and Finlayson completed their master plan for UTM, collective thinking had shifted to ecological performance and a more incremental approach to building, underscored by the concept of landscape as the connective, community-making tissue. Sterling and Finlayson's campus plan established an intelligent framework for development and expansion at UTM and received a City of Mississauga Urban Design Award in 2005.

Remarkable growth and change have unfolded over the past four decades. As its founders imagined from the start, UTM is commuter-intensive, but there are now diverse living options on campus. In addition to the town-house clusters, three new residence halls have recently been realized, bringing the total on-campus accommodations to more than one thousand four hundred beds. The recent completions of an interdisciplinary academic building, a library/learning center, and a recreation/athletic center—along with a surge in construction of housing for students—have dramatically changed the feel of UTM. During the past ten years the campus has transformed from a loose agglomeration of structures to a bustling villagelike place. If not highly integrated in the Andrews and Moriyama modes, UTM has nevertheless become a vibrant intellectual and social campus.

This architectural transformation seems particularly significant and timely in the context of the rapid growth of Mississauga. UTM is a sophisticated anchor in this sprawling city of seven hundred thousand, Canada's sixth largest. Created in 1974 from a disparate collection of small towns, Mississauga has become a bizarre, highly complex urban-suburban landscape that struggles to retain remnants of its original geography and social history. Indeed, only a few hundred years have passed since first Iroquois, then Mississauga peoples, and, later, French trappers lived along the winding Credit River, above which UTM's modern campus is now perched.

Alumni House

99. Alumni House *David R. Franklin, 1922*

This unassuming structure was completed in 1922 as a public school. It was designed in the colonial revival style by David R. Franklin, a Toronto architect who specialized in school buildings. Undistinguished wings were added in 1952 to accommodate the growing number of children in the Erindale community. It became the Springbank Community Centre in 1957 and the home of Visual Arts Mississauga in 1962.

The university purchased the building, which is located adjacent to the main entrance to the campus, in 2003. UTM originally planned to convert it to an alumni and visitors center, but this notion was abandoned, and it now temporarily houses parking and business services until more suitable uses are determined. Recognizing its architectural and historic significance, the Ontario Heritage Act designated the building in 1974, and the City of Mississauga and UTM are planning to restore many of its original exterior and interior features.

South Building

100. South Building

Phase One: Research and Laboratory Block (J. Tuzo Wilson Research Wing) *A. D. Margison & Associates with Raymond Moriyama as design consultant, 1971*

Phase Two: Library, Lecture, Theatre Complex
A. D. Margison & Associates, 1973

Phase Three: Centre for Applied Biosciences and Biotechnology (CABB)
Stantec Architecture Ltd., 2002

Arriving from Mississauga Road and either the main or middle entrance to campus, one encounters a large pond. Just beyond is the South Building, which serves as the front door to the campus. Derived from a vast, megastructural concept by architect Raymond Moriyama, the South Building is constructed of reinforced concrete and presents an aggressive expression of horizontal and vertical circulation elements and, in Phase One, of laboratory ducting systems. The 1971 Research and Laboratory Block is architecturally accomplished, employing sculpted forms and a robust material palette. The softly curved towers, which house the stairs; naturally lit corridors; recessed wooden window frames; rugged pine railings; and rust-colored clay tiles covering the walls of the corridors combine to create a visceral interior environment that is rewarding to the senses.

Phase Two (originally the Library, Lecture, Theatre Complex) architecturally mimics Phase One, but, with its painted concrete-block walls, feels like a poor cousin. This portion of the South Building served for thirty years as the center of campus life and contains classrooms, a library, a bookstore, health services, food services, counseling areas, athletic facilities, and the central "Meeting Place" that was and continues to be a gathering point for commuters. UTM's main administrative offices are on the second floor.

In 2002 UTM completed a small yet elegant addition to the South Building, the Centre for Applied Biosciences and Biotechnology (CABB), which provides specialized biotech facilities for twenty faculty and eighty graduate and doctoral students. It houses research on combining the precision of DNA chemistry with the speed of fiber optics, leading to rapid testing and screening for life-threatening infections and diseases such as hepatitis and AIDS. The de Stijl-like composition of the CABB recalls the 1924 Rietveld Schröder House in Utrecht designed by Gerrit Rietveld, but dressed up, rather heavily and mysteriously, in a cloak of charcoal black. This small wing is able to hold its own next to the giant alongside it.

In recent years, the university has started breaking up the bulk of the South Building—which continues to be a somewhat perplexing maze—with the creation of through-routes and linkages to other structures. New connections to the Recreation, Athletics and Wellness Centre to the southeast and to the Communication, Culture and Technology Building at the northwest are welcome improvements. A band of bluish solar panels added to the south face of the building signify its ongoing revitalization.

101. Kaneff Centre *Shore Tilbe Henschel Irwin Peters, 1992*

Opened in 1992 as the Kaneff Centre for Management and Social Studies, this building seems at first glance rather humdrum and without architectural merit. The fenestration is uninteresting, and the aqua-colored aluminum window frames are typical of commercial architecture in the late 1980s and early 1990s. Aside from it politely lining up with the front of the nearby South Building, the Kaneff Centre stands alone, with no easily discernable relationship to nearby structures.

The center presents a surprising and different story inside, though. The building's square footprint has a large circular space 120 feet in diameter cut into it, forming an outdoor courtyard that opens to the east. A pleasant, light-filled interior circulation corridor wraps around and overlooks the circle. Although the cylindrical courtyard seems unfinished, waiting for a landscape solution that could activate it visually and socially, it does embody a protourbanity that UTM has been incrementally embracing. In this regard the fifteen-year-old Kaneff Centre might be seen as the new kid on the block that challenged the campus's ingrained suburban mentality.

Kaneff Centre

The ambitious Blackwood Gallery, housed in the Kaneff Centre, is named to honor Canadian artist David Blackwood, who was appointed in 1969 as the first artist-in-residence at UTM (then Erindale College). The Blackwood Gallery has become a major player in the Toronto art scene, hosting exhibitions of leading contemporary artists.

102. Communication, Culture and Technology (CCT) Building   *Saucier + Perrotte, 2004*

Simply stated, the CCT interdisciplinary community asks: How can communication, in all its dimensions, build knowledge and create culture? The elegant, minimalist structure that houses the CCT program provides a suitably provocative environment for engaging intellectual questions such as this.

The T-shaped, four-story CCT Building comprises nearly 113,000 square feet (10,500 square meters) and contains interactive computer classrooms and laboratories, editing suites, faculty offices, a multimedia studio theater, a 500-seat lecture theater, an e-gallery for electronic art exhibitions, and underground parking. It also houses the Human Communication Lab and the Institute of Communication and Culture. The building created two new courtyards and links the South Building and the heart of the campus northeastward to the Hazel McCallion Academic Learning Centre. With its parallel pedestrian "streets"—one outdoors, one indoors—straddling a reflective glass wall, it is experientially reminiscent of the mirrored environments created by artists such as Lucas Samaras. The magnificently sculpted northeast facade—which has hard-edge glass boxes that weave in and out of it, and also incorporates strips of mirror—demonstrates how architecture can both embrace notions of movement and be simultaneously solid and transparent.

Inside is a monumentally scaled commons area that, in its highly controlled spatial complexity, is reminiscent of the soaring, mysterious spaces of the eighteenth-century Roman architect-theorist Giovanni Battista Piranesi. In the CCT Building, though, Montreal-based architects Saucier + Perrotte also offer contrasting intimate spaces, and the whole design is joined together by a cool palette of black, white, and gray.

The greatest success of the CCT Building is its strong integration with adjacent structures and the surrounding landscape. This is particularly apparent at the south and east areas of the building, where the folded planes of an expressive black auditorium mirror a series of folded, grass-covered ground planes. Saucier + Perrotte have developed a sophisticated understanding of landscape, both natural and artificial, that enables them to generate an architecture that is abstract and universal but also deeply embedded in the particulars of a specific place. From this, they seek what they refer to as a building's "soul," which they clearly found in the CCT Building.

Indeed, it is not surprising that the building won the Ordre des Architectes du Québec Award for Best Institutional Building in 2007, an Ontario Association of Architects Award of Excellence in 2007, and a Governor General of Canada Award in 2008. It is the most striking of the eight new structures realized at UTM since 1999 and sets an appropriately high benchmark for future projects.

103. Recreation, Athletics and Wellness Centre (RAWC)
Shore Tilbe Irwin & Partners, 2006

The university recently added the Recreation, Athletics and Wellness Centre (RAWC), an efficient recreation and athletics complex, onto the South Building, fully integrating the two spaces and generating a new southeast gateway into the campus from the adjacent parking lots. A granite-paved grand stair that rises through three levels signifies this gateway condition and unifies the RAWC with the South Building.

The architects employed multiple transparencies to provide visual connections between the building's various gymnasia, Olympic-class swimming pool, and running track. On a typical day the facility is abuzz with activity, presenting a scene of bodies moving through and engaging the architectural space. With simple means, the design creates a recreational/athletic machine that recalls the social goals of

Communication, Culture and Technology Building

Recreation, Athletics and Wellness Centre

health and well-being promoted by early-twentieth-century modernist architects such as Le Corbusier.

A planted green roof covers the swimming pool volume, which, to the northwest, lends a defining edge to a series of terraces that step up from the RAWC to the South Building.

104. Hazel McCallion Academic Learning Centre
Shore Tilbe Irwin & Partners, 2006

This recent addition to UTM is named in honor of Hazel McCallion, the mayor of Mississauga. Hazel, as she is affectionately called by her admirers, has served as mayor for the past thirty years and celebrated her eighty-seventh birthday in early 2008. She has been an unwavering champion and booster for UTM, so it is fitting that the university's new library bears the name of this energetic woman who has led the city so successfully.

The architects based the four-story building's design for a technically driven, information-obsessed society on the concept of an architectural "puzzle box," where users open the box to discover an inner cabinet of stored knowledge (both print and digital). Moveable sliding units of compact shelving efficiently accommodate the library's entire collection of print material. The facade's interplay of rectilinear volumes, alternating between Prodema wood-veneer panels and large glazed areas with bluish glass fins, represents the puzzle box notion. Within this box, light wells bring sunlight deep into the library's interior and introduce dynamic diagonal views. A long study counter along the northwest side of the building is popular with students.

Hazel McCallion Academic Learning Centre

A glazed passageway links the Academic Learning Centre to the CCT Building to the southwest. Along this route one can glimpse handsomely landscaped courtyards and a lovely wooded area that is particularly spectacular in the fall, when the red, orange, and yellow leaves complement the library's reddish brown cladding.

105. Student Centre *Kohn Shnier Architects, 1999*

The Student Centre resulted from a 1996/97 national design competition that garnered more than one hundred entries and launched the architectural renaissance that UTM has enjoyed for the past ten years. Kohn Shnier Architects won the competition with a rigorous design that functions as a gateway for the "Five Minute Walk," the route between the central academic buildings and the wooded area to the northeast where most of the student residences are.

The centre contains student clubs, the campus radio station CFRE, newspaper and student union offices, lounges, a restaurant/pub, a multifaith prayer room, and generous outdoor areas—all nestled under a butterfly roof. The architects organized the building into four horizontal bands: restaurant/pub, multipurpose rooms, linear lobby/lounge, and student activity offices. Within each of these bands there is flexibility to adjust programs and activities, and there is also functional flexibility between the bands. The competition brief required an existing two-story retail structure, the Crossroads Building, to be incorporated into the new project, and Kohn Shnier used it as their fourth band, the student activity offices.

A dramatic red fireplace lounge and an elegant white music room face the forest and provide contained counterpoints within the building's otherwise networklike composition. The minimalist restaurant/pub space—with tall walls of glass forming

Student Centre

North Building

three of its sides—was immediately controversial, seen by some students as too exposed, too public. Partly because of this, students altered the space to be more "rec room"-like and cozy, without seeking much guidance from the architects. Other areas of the building have been modified haphazardly in recent years, including the covered terrace along the south facade. These changes have undermined the Student Centre's minimalist, modernist verve, which brought it international attention at the end of the twentieth century. Nevertheless, the architects' conceptual banding has survived and enables waves of student life to flex robustly into the twenty-first century.

106. North Building *Levine & Lawrence, 1967*
Addition *G. Edwards Lutman, 1969*

The North Building was the first new structure built after the founding of Erindale College, referred to on early drawings simply as "Olympia York," a shorthand reference to Olympia and York, the Toronto-based property development firm founded in the early 1950s by the Reichmann brothers that assisted with the project. Originally intended as a small administrative headquarters, the North Building was expanded in 1969 when construction of the main South Building was delayed. From certain angles, its walls of repetitive, vertical precast concrete panels and fins transcend monotony, appearing windowless and highly abstract. The North Building continues to serve as a major academic building, housing humanities disciplines and anthropology and acting as a gateway to the campus at the northern edge.

Roy Ivor Hall

107. Roy Ivor Hall
*Baird Sampson Neuert Architects in joint venture with Fliess Gates
McGowan Easton Architects Inc., 1999*

Roy Ivor Hall, a residence for 190 students, is loosely based on the Oxford college model. It is organized into four volumetrically distinct house clusters, each with its own stair. The typical living arrangement consists of an apartment with four bedrooms. The site plan preserved mature trees, and the building focuses on a garden of indigenous plants surrounding a small pond. Realized on a modest budget, Roy Ivor Hall is impressive for its imaginative embedding in the landscape (which takes advantage of subtle topographical shifts), gentle humanizing scale, handsome materials palette, and tectonic rigor.

The building's concept flows from an approach that balances Bauhaus-like rationality (note, for example, the large, thoughtfully designed windows in student rooms that provide ample light and pleasant views) with phenomenological preoccupations that owe something to Frank Lloyd Wright and Canadian architect Ron Thom. What results is an intricate architectural composition with a strong sense of context.

Roy Ivor Hall's varied material and color palette—iron-flecked orange-brown brick, blue-gray slate tile, red-brown horizontally corrugated steel panels—is masterfully orchestrated and proportioned. It can be argued that less is not always more,

Erindale Hall

and the visual complexity of the building makes a convincing case for this statement, its textures merging with the surrounding landscape.

In terms of urban design, Roy Ivor Hall is intelligently resolved, presenting a long and regular rhythm along Mississauga Road, while communicating a looser, picturesque quality from Residence Road on the campus side. The complex also kindly engages the Schreiberwood townhouses to the north. In 2004 Roy Ivor Hall won both an Ontario Association of Architects Award of Excellence and a City of Mississauga Urban Design Award of Excellence.

The residence was touchingly named for the "Bird Man of Mississauga," Roy Ivor, who lived in a mobile home in the woods across from the campus. He took in and cured injured birds and created a sanctuary for them.

108. Erindale Hall *Baird Sampson Neuert Architects, 2005*

The name of this two hundred-student residence honors the campus's transition from Erindale College to the University of Toronto Mississauga. The curved primary volume—which parallels and reinforces the Five Minute Walk—consists of a long "bar building" supported by nineteen V-shaped *pilotis* that form the edge of a colonnade. The meandering back wall of the colonnade is faced in alternating zones of coarse, fissured capstone (removed in the quarrying of Algonquin limestone) and sleek, mullionless glass; overhead hangs a rhythmic soffit with lighting slots cut into it and finished with delicate blue ceramic tiles. At the bend in the slender bar building, a small entrance foyer is glazed on both sides to provide views of the surrounding wooded areas, which are protected ecological zones. The roofs of the building collect rainwater, which is used to recharge adjacent wetland. The east, convex side of Erindale Hall has three five-story residence towers branching out from the main bar building. Between these towers, in the primary volume, run carefully detailed glazed corridors. Many aspects of this handsome building are reminiscent of the work of the modernist architects Le Corbusier and Alvar Aalto, from the spirited *pilotis* to the sophisticated material palette.

109. Oscar Peterson Hall *Cannon Design, 2007*

Oscar Peterson Hall

This residence hall, UTM's newest, honors Oscar Peterson, the late Canadian jazz musician and longtime resident of Mississauga. The largest residence on campus, it accommodates over 420 students, who are housed in suites comprised of two bedrooms that share a bathroom. Oscar Peterson Hall also houses the Colman Commons, a food court for all UTM residences.

The building is sited in the center of the heavily wooded western sector of the campus, facing Roy Ivor Hall and backing onto Erindale Hall. It is S-shaped, generating a courtyard directly across from Roy Ivor Hall's pond and garden. Given the careful siting strategies and architectural sophistication of the earlier Ivor and Erindale residences, which are gently tucked into their sites, it is both surprising and regrettable that the university seemed to lose architectural focus and courage in the realization of Oscar Peterson Hall. This five- and six-story brick-clad dorm feels too large for its site, and there is little tectonic finesse.

110. Lislehurst *Herbert Harrie Schreiber, builder, 1885*
Renovation *Reginald Watkins, 1928*

Lislehurst is the gracious home of the principal of UTM. Nestled deep in the heavily wooded area at the north end of the campus, it was built of Credit Valley stone in 1885 by the Schreiber family, who hailed from England and were descendants

TOP: *Lislehurst*
BOTTOM: *Lislehurst Bridge*

of Sir Isaac Brock. (There were originally three Schreiber houses in the area, but, other than traces of foundations, only Lislehurst remains.) A subsequent owner, Reginald Watkins, a Hamilton businessman, renovated the house in 1928, adding a large wing to the west. The property became known as the Watkins Estate and was purchased by the University of Toronto in the mid-1960s to create the new Erindale College campus. Lislehurst is designated under the Ontario Heritage Act, recognized for its architectural and historical importance.

Inside, the house exudes English country coziness, from the wood beams in the entrance hall to an array of exquisite fireplaces to the deer that frequently pass by and peer through the living room windows. Throughout hang lovely etchings and paintings by Charlotte Mount Brock Schreiber, wife of Herbert and an accomplished artist. Do not miss the delightful Lislehurst Bridge, not far from the historic home and a popular spot for wedding photographs.

111. Health Sciences Complex
Kongats Architects, expected completion 2010

In 2006, when the province of Ontario approved the expansion of medical programs, including the University of Toronto's Faculty of Medicine's expansion to the Mississauga campus, a UTM medical academy was created in conjunction with local hospitals. This academy will occupy two-thirds of the new Health Sciences Complex, which is under construction to the northeast of the South Building and to the southeast of the CCT Building. The new structure will consist of four stories, each level designed as a sculptural "programmatic box" that expresses its internal function (first floor = lecture halls; second floor = seminar rooms; third floor = offices; fourth floor = laboratories). These stacked boxes are offset to create outdoor, landscaped decks and terraces. The box volumes are clad in vertical stainless steel panels that also act as louvers or fins, and will generate a varied facade that ranges from opaque to transparent.

Renderings of Health Sciences Complex

Walk Nine: University of Toronto Off Campus and Surroundings

This last walk focuses on four of the University of Toronto's off-campus buildings and fourteen architecturally noteworthy buildings in the immediate area around the downtown St. George campus. The latter span from Richard A. Waite's Ontario Legislative Building of 1892 to Frank Gehry's Art Gallery of Ontario, completed in 2008. They not only present an engaging cross-section of 116 years of Toronto architectural history but also serve as a reminder of how tastes change and styles come and go, and that controversy and scandal in the world of architecture are nothing new.

Most importantly, these diverse buildings reveal the city's long tradition of architectural innovation and excellence, something that Torontonians tend to overlook or even deny. These formidable works of architecture constitute an appropriate final footnote. They complement the university buildings and places presented earlier in this guide and underscore the rich cultural relationships and flow of ideas that exist between town and gown.

112. President's House, 93 Highland Avenue
Wickson & Gregg, 1910

This home in Toronto's Rosedale neighborhood is attributed to the firm of Wickson & Gregg, which was formed in 1905 and designed nearly forty large residences in Toronto. The president's house was originally built for David Alexander Dunlap, a gold-mining magnate whose philanthropist wife, Jessie, donated the David Dunlap Observatory to the University in 1935, honoring her husband. (The university sold the observatory in 2008.)

President's House

Institute of Child Study

In 1956 the university purchased Dunlap mansion to serve as the official residence for the president and for entertaining. University social occasions are gracefully accommodated in the sophisticated sequence of spaces that the house provides. From a porte-cochere, guests enter a vestibule leading to an elegant receiving room, off of which are a formal yet intimate dining room with ornate plaster work, a paneled library, and a large living room with an adjacent, plant-filled solarium. The rear of the house opens onto extensive lawns and gardens. Perched above one of Toronto's twenty-nine ravines, the President's House offers magnificent views to the downtown skyline.

113. Institute of Child Study, 45 Walmer Road

Sproatt & Rolph, 1932
Addition *Gordon Adamson & Associates, date unknown*

The Institute of Child Study (ICS), which is part of the Ontario Institute for Studies in Education, contributes to the knowledge and understanding of child development. It evolved from the St. George's School of Child Study, established in 1925 by Edward Bott, the first head of psychology at the University of Toronto. During the 1930s, the St. George's School came into national and international prominence for its role in the early education of the Dionne quintuplets. The school also became an important contributor to Canada's war effort, helping to establish war nurseries in England. The Georgian-style house that accommodates the ICS was designed by the talented Henry Sproatt and was one of his last works before he died in 1934. The home originally belonged to the Hon. Leighton Goldie McCarthy, who donated it to the university in 1955.

114. 89 Chestnut Residence *Armstrong & Molesworth, 1971*

89 Chestnut Residence

Located next door to Toronto City Hall, this former hotel was purchased by the university in 2003 and adapted as a residence accommodating 950 students. It was originally the Civic Square Holiday Inn, touted as "the largest Holiday Inn in the world with 750 luxury rooms and suites." Its twenty-seventh floor deluxe eatery, La Ronde, was the city's only revolving restaurant until the CN Tower opened in 1976.

The concrete-clad building consists of a twenty-four-floor tower rising from a three-story podium that is linked by a bridge to the podium of City Hall. The facades of the tower present a grid of alternating pairs of windows and tiny recessed balconies.

115. The Koffler Scientific Reserve at Joker's Hill, 17000 Dufferin Street

Principal residence *Mathers & Haldenby, 1953*
Renovation of principal residence *B. Napier Simpson, Jr., late 1960s to early 1970s*
Gazebo *Raymond Moriyama, 1972*

It is not generally well known that the university owns a spectacular 860-acre property (formerly a horse farm) an hour north of Toronto. Situated in King Township in the west portion of the Oak Ridges Moraine, Joker's Hill, as the horse farm was called, was generously donated to the university by Murray and Marvelle Koffler in 1995. Recognizing the biological and geological diversity of the area, the university established a scientific research station at Joker's Hill in 2002 and uses this significant environmental landscape for teaching and research.

The original building at Joker's Hill was designed by Mathers & Haldenby and completed around 1952. It was a rambling, wood-clad ranch-style house, built for General C. Churchill Mann and his wife, Billie Mann, the second owners of the property. Billie Mann was the daughter of the original owner, Colonel R. S.

The Koffler Scientific Reserve

McLaughlin, founder of the automobile industry in Canada and breeder of champion thoroughbred race horses.

When the Kofflers bought the farm in 1969, they commissioned the noted Canadian architect B. Napier Simpson, Jr. to renovate and add to the house. He completely transformed it, adding grand extensions that created a U-shaped courtyard accommodating a swimming pool. The house is a good example of Simpson's signature use of locally sourced material, such as wood, stone, iron, slate, and barn board, which, through his rhythmic and imaginative manipulation, generates a unified architectural vocabulary.

The couple also engaged landscape architect J. Austin Floyd, one of Canada's first modern landscape architects, to redesign the grounds and reshape the ponds on the property; and commissioned Raymond Moriyama to design a chaletlike recreational structure on the edge of one of the ponds. Known as "the gazebo," it is playful yet elegant. The rugged wood structure focuses on a 360-degree stone fire hearth and surrounding table with a copper-clad hood. Rising from this is a chimney, which penetrates the peak of the roof and the center of a double-glazed skylight. Although modest, the gazebo remains one of Moriyama's most charming structures.

The manor house and its surrounding landscape constitute an important part of Ontario's heritage. Indeed, Joker's Hill, now protected by the Oak Ridges Moraine Conservation Act, has become a significant oasis of green and calm amidst the alarming urban sprawl creeping northward from Toronto.

116. Toronto Athletic Club (Stewart Building), 149 College Street *E. J. Lennox, 1894*

Toronto Athletic Club

Constructed on what had been cricket grounds in the nineteenth century, the Toronto Athletic Club, also known as the Stewart Building, was originally equipped with a gymnasium, dining rooms, a room dedicated to the card game of whist, and the city's first indoor swimming pool. Although its original front steps were crudely replaced, and the building today sits in a sea of asphalt-paved parking lots, this Richardsonian Romanesque, palazzo-like structure retains much of its original grandeur.

Its architect, Edward James Lennox, better known as E. J. Lennox, was responsible

Gardiner Museum (during 2006 construction)

for many important Ontario buildings, including the Toronto City Hall (opened in 1899 and now called Old City Hall), the King Edward Hotel of 1903, the flamboyant Casa Loma residence of 1911, and the monumental Toronto Power Generating Station at Niagara Falls, finished in 1913.

The Stewart Building has housed numerous institutions and organizations over the years, including the Central Technical School, 52 Division Toronto Police, College du Grand Lacs, and the Ontario College of Art and Design, which owned the building from 1979 to 1997, using it as a second campus.

117. Gardiner Museum, 111 Queen's Park
Keith Wagland, 1984
Renovation and additions *Kuwabara Payne McKenna Blumberg Architects, 2006*

George and Helen Gardiner opened the Gardiner Museum in 1984 to house their collection of ancient American artifacts and European pottery and porcelain. Located on Victoria University lands, it was recently redesigned by Kuwabara Payne McKenna Blumberg Architects, who wanted to "give this great small

The Ontario Legislative Building

museum an intimate monumentality," as Bruce Kuwabara stated. Rising from a series of terraced platforms, the hovering limestone-clad building consists of a composition of cubic volumes, accented by a bold screen of limestone louvers. The interior spatial sequence is gentle, flowing up to a third-floor gallery for temporary exhibitions, an exquisite restaurant, and a terrace with wonderful vistas of Queen's Park, the Royal Ontario Museum, the University of Toronto, and the downtown skyline.

In scale and character, the museum negotiates between the austerity of the neoclassical Lillian Massey Department of Household Science on the north and the Queen Anne–style Annesley Hall on the south. The three now sit together comfortably, demonstrating how historical and contemporary buildings can be successfully related.

118. The Ontario Legislative Building (Queen's Park)
Richard A. Waite, 1892
Rebuilding of west wing *E. J. Lennox, 1912*
North library addition *George W. Gouinlock, 1910*

In Toronto the term "Queen's Park" applies to many things: a large urban park, a street, a subway station, the dozen or so buildings housing the offices of the province of Ontario, and the Ontario Legislative Building at the head of University Avenue. Even the provincial government is casually called "Queen's Park." The park itself, named in honor of Queen Victoria, was planned by Edwin Taylor, an English landscape gardener who had trained with Sir Joseph Paxton, and was completed in 1860. Before the crude traffic overpass was constructed at the southwest corner in the 1950s, the urban space of Queen's Park flowed unencumbered into the University of Toronto campus, past Hart House, to King's College Circle.

The other "Queen's Park," the imposing, pink stone Ontario Legislative Building, was completed in 1892 on the site of the former King's College (demolished in 1886; see pages 11 to 12). It took from 1852, when Cumberland and Storm won a competition for a building on the King's College site, to 1892–forty years of angst, wrangling, and aborted attempts–before a new legislative building was finally built. Even though the provincial government proceeded to dismantle King's College, they refused to commit money for Cumberland & Storm's building. Designs by government architect Kivas Tully were advanced in 1877 and 1880 but, again, nothing happened. Finally, an international competition was held in 1880, and the jury favored two entries by Darling & Curry and Smith & Gemmell, only to discover that both greatly exceeded the declared budget. The government revived the building project in 1885, raising the budget to $750,000 and calling on one of the jury members, Buffalo architect Richard A. Waite, to decide between the two designs. Waite declared both defective. Then, incredibly, the government appointed Waite himself to design the new legislative building. Construction commenced in 1886, and the building was completed in 1892, costing nearly $1,400,000.

Waite's Romanesque-revival design is organized in a U-shape, with the legislative chamber at the center, on the second floor. Four domed turrets flank a steep slate roof, and side wings with galleried halls extend to the east and west, each terminated by round-arched porte cocheres. The interiors, detailed with carved wood and cast and wrought iron, are sumptuous. Following a 1909 fire, the west wing was rebuilt by E. J. Lennox, and George W. Gouinlock designed the north library wing completed in 1910. The north entrance to the library (on Wellesley Street)–a beautiful Romanesque portal–incorporates an Ontario coat of arms and realistically sculpted animals (a moose, deer, and bear).

A throned Queen Victoria, sculpted by Mario Raggi (1903), is positioned at the southeast corner of the building. She seems content with the architecture behind her, unprovoked by the bickering and lavish budget overruns that surrounded Waite's appointment and the construction of this place more than a century ago. Maybe she is simply happy that everything around her is, rather strangely, "Queen's Park."

119. One St. Thomas Residences, One St. Thomas Street
Robert A. M. Stern Architects, 2008

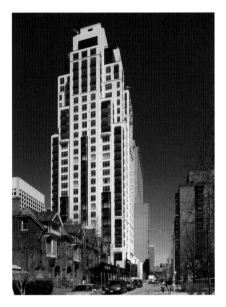

One St. Thomas Residences

During this first decade of the twenty-first century, Toronto has spawned hundreds of condominium towers, and in North America the city now ranks second to New York in the number of people living in high-rise buildings. Architecturally, the dramatic "verticalization" of Toronto has been a mixed blessing, with few truly beautiful residential towers added to the urban fabric. A notable exception to the proliferation of architectural mediocrity is the creamy-white, twenty-nine-story luxury tower on St. Thomas Street by Robert A. M. Stern. Stern is a native New Yorker, author of *New York 1960: Architecture and Urbanism Between the Second World War and the Bicentennial*, and Dean of the Yale School of Architecture, so it comes as no surprise that the urbane architect has taken cues from the grand era of New York apartment buildings, the 1920s and 1930s, and translated them into an eye-catching, stepped high-rise for Toronto, anchored at the base by a porte cochere, formal garden, and wing of elegant townhouses running eastward. A sculpted marble wall by artist Carl Tacon graces the driveway along the north.

The stepped silhouette of Stern's design is interesting to observe from a few blocks south, in relation to the 1933 Whitney Block tower at Queen's Park, which is similarly stepped and exquisitely detailed.

120. The Colonnade, 131 Bloor Street West
Gerald Robinson Architect (with Tampold & Wells), 1964

Among many factors contributing to Toronto's success as a dynamic, contemporary city is its array of "mixed-use" buildings—structures that have more than one use and that, typically, mix these uses for economic and social advantage. The Colonnade, which encompasses luxury apartments, retail shops, restaurants, offices, and a parking garage, was completed in 1964 on land owned by Victoria University and was one of Toronto's first ambitiously mixed-use buildings. It recalls many of

The Colonnade

the intentions of Le Corbusier's Unité d'Habitation in Marseilles, completed just twelve years earlier.

The upper apartment volume, which includes over 160 apartments, presents a screenlike facade of concrete, made of dominant horizontals punctuated with a rapid rhythm of short verticals. This volume rests on a podium that houses publicly accessible offices, shops, and restaurants. Along Bloor Street, this podium is convincingly inflected to form a semicircular plaza and welcoming entry. The second-floor shopping area has ample height and a sectional development that brings in generous amounts of natural light.

121. The Royal Ontario Museum, 100 Queens Park

Darling & Pearson, 1914; Chapman & Oxley, 1933; Moffat Moffat & Kinoshita, 1984

McLaughlin Planetarium *Allward & Gouinlock Architects, 1968*

Michael Lee-Chin Crystal *Studio Daniel Libeskind with Bregman + Hamman Architects, 2007*

The Royal Ontario Museum (ROM) is the largest museum in Canada and one of the world's preeminent centers for the exhibition and study of world cultures and natural history, with a collection of more than six million items. Established in 1912 by the province's Royal Ontario Museum Act, the ROM was operated by the University of Toronto until 1968. It is now an independent institution but maintains close ties with the university and is located at the northeast corner of the St. George campus.

Darling and Pearson's master plan for ROM had a rectangular plan with two huge rectangular courts carved out of the massive volume. About a quarter of this beaux arts–inspired design was realized in 1914, along the western edge of the site (see page 26). In 1933 Chapman & Oxley completed a large T-shaped addition, fronting on Queen's Park, which gave the museum an overall H-shape. Following this, Darling & Pearson's master plan was abandoned: the area they had imagined to be a grand south court was filled in with a massive curatorial building, and their proposed grand north court was used for a gallery addition terracing down to Bloor Street. This 1984 infilling was only the most flagrant of hundreds of incremental erasures of the original intentions and clarity of Darling & Pearson's vision. The architecture suffered through the insertion of mechanical rooms, the covering of windows, and the division of galleries, which gradually led to visual and experiential

The Royal Ontario Museum

confusion for museum visitors. A key aspect of architect Daniel Libeskind's 2007 redesign of the ROM has been to clean up and clear out the bothersome clutter of the past several decades (including the 1984 north addition), restoring much of the clarity of Darling & Pearson's and Chapman & Oxley's designs.

It is Libeskind's bold metallic crystal addition on Bloor Street, called the Michael Lee-Chin Crystal after its main donor, that commands the most attention, however. The architect originally proposed to cover about 50 percent of the building with glass or some kind of translucent material, but due to climatic and curatorial pressures the surface glazing had to be reduced to about 20 percent, a change that remains disappointing. The interior spaces are dramatic and engaging, though, particularly the soaring Hyacinth Gloria Chen Crystal Court, which finally completes, at least conceptually, the north court where Darling & Pearson had imagined it. The Crystal Court is a monumental space, topped by two mysterious, shardlike skylights and has become one of the city's great rooms—a coveted venue for receptions, experimental art installations and cultural performances. Equally impressive is the fifth-floor restaurant that extends, prowlike, over the 1914 building and has an imaginative new adjacent roof garden by the Toronto architect-landscape group PLANT Architect, Inc.

The ROM also owns the former McLaughlin Planetarium (closed in 1995), located at the south end of its property. In 2005 a forty-six-story condominium was designed to replace the planetarium but was deemed by some to be out of scale and an inappropriate use, given the adjacency of the site to Philosopher's Walk and the University of Toronto faculties of law and music. The ROM is now working to generate a more sympathetic solution for the development of the planetarium site.

The Royal Conservatory of Music

122. The Royal Conservatory of Music and the TELUS Centre for Performance and Learning, 273 Bloor Street West

Baptist Theological College *Langley, Langley & Burke, 1882*
Castle Memorial Hall *Burke & Horwood, 1901*
Science Hall *Burke & Horwood, 1907 (demolished 2002)*
Renovation and additions *Kuwabara Payne McKenna Blumberg Architects, 1997, 2009*

Founded in 1886 as the Toronto Conservatory of Music, this venerable institution (which counts Glenn Gould among its graduates) has been located at 273 Bloor Street West since 1962 and gained independence from the University of Toronto in 1991. Tightly bounded by the Royal Ontario Museum and Philosopher's Walk on the east and the university's Varsity Centre at the south and west, the conservatory has been engaged in a ten-year program of expansion and renovation that binds together its magnificent Victorian fabric with sympathetic contemporary additions. Due to the small site, Kuwabara Payne McKenna Blumberg Architects also had to make sacrifices, including the demolition of the fine south wing and stair tower of the original 1882 building by Langley, Langley & Burke.

Bata Shoe Museum

The revitalized complex centers around historic McMaster Hall (originally the Baptist Theological College, then McMaster University) and features three concert spaces: Mazzoleni Hall; a new Rehearsal Hall; and a new classic "shoebox," one thousand-seat Concert Hall. The latter is positioned east-west, floating over the west edge of Philosopher's Walk and grafted onto McMaster Hall with a dramatic sky-lit court.

One of the most successful aspects of the reborn conservatory is the forecourt along Bloor Street West, framed on the west by Mazzoleni Hall, at the south by McMaster Hall, and on the west by a new entrance pavilion. The wing containing the new entrance is boldly scaled and colored, smoothly fitting in with the heritage structure while refusing to kowtow to history. Together, these elements create a pleasing public urban space.

123. Bata Shoe Museum, 327 Bloor Street West
Moriyama & Teshima Architects, 1995

The Bata Shoe Museum is the brainchild of Sonja Bata, wife of Thomas J. Bata, whose father Tomas Bata established the Bata Shoe Company in the Moravian Czech town of Zlin in 1894. Between 1931 and 1939 the Bata company expanded widely throughout Europe, Asia, Africa, and the Americas. It adhered to progressive planning, emulated Ebenezer Howard's garden city ideals, and aggressively embraced modern architecture for its factories, offices, stores, and workers'

The York Club

housing. The prominent Canadian architect John C. Parkin designed Bata's world headquarters in Don Mills, Ontario, completed in 1965 and recognized as one of Toronto's most important mid-century modern buildings (demolished in 2007).

Trained in Switzerland as an architect herself, Sonja Bata commissioned Raymond Moriyama to design the five-story Bata Shoe Museum, which contains some 10,000 artifacts spanning 4,500 years of footwear history. The museum fits neatly into a tight urban site with three floors above ground and two below. The building's canted walls and glass-shard elements suggest influence from the Museum of Modern Art's 1988 exhibition "Deconstructivist Architecture." Perhaps it is also meant to evoke an opening shoe box. Inside, a multilevel spatial cut contains the main stair and provides a clear view to the three-story faceted glass wall designed by Lutz Haufschild on the south facade.

124. The York Club, 135 St. George Street
David Roberts, Jr., 1892

What is now the prestigious York Club was once a private mansion built for George Gooderham, president of the Gooderham and Worts distillery, a complex of buildings at the east edge of downtown that have been recently restored and christened the Distillery District. After Gooderham's death in 1905, the York Club purchased the mansion in 1908, and the university's board of governors often held meetings there. It remains one of the best examples of Romanesque-revival architecture in Toronto.

The geometrically complex, luxuriant structure is anchored by a muscular tower on the southwest corner and presents strong facades on both St. George and Bloor streets. To the right of the front door, the carved ornament includes a portrait of Henry Sproatt, who worked on the design with Roberts and who later was one of the architects of the university's Hart House.

Constructed of red stone, brick, and terra-cotta, the York Club is a landmark in the city's Annex district. With the construction of numerous new condominium towers nearby, along Bloor Street West, and given the increasing densification of Toronto, the York Club and its gardens are a reminder of the key importance of both human scale and robust color and texture in urban environments.

125. Lord Lansdowne Public School, 33 Robert Street
Frederick C. Etherington, 1961

Lord Lansdowne Public School

The Lord Landsdowne Public School presents a striking image on the corners of Robert Street and Spadina Crescent. What is this spiky eruption? A former world's fair pavilion? A lost fragment of Sputnik? Whatever one's reading of the building, it is fortunate that this exuberant work of modern architecture from 1961 not only still exists but continues to provide a stimulating environment for some 340 students.

The school is knit together of steel, concrete, concrete block, brick, and metal. However, it is the very slender steel pylons supporting a circular, folded roof that grab so much attention and make the building memorable. The sculpted pylons also define a kind of dramatic porch that flows around the central classroom pavilion.

Frederick C. Etherington, who graduated from the Ontario College of Art and apprenticed with the Toronto firm of Sproatt and Rolph, was the imaginative architect of the project. He was appointed chief architect of the Toronto Board of Education in 1951 and continued in that position until his retirement in 1965.

At a time when Toronto is losing so many fine mid-twentieth-century works of architecture, one can only hope that the Lord Landsdowne Public School will continue to be appreciated and preserved.

126. Lillian H. Smith Branch Library, 239 College Street

Phillip H. Carter, 1995

Lillian H. Smith Branch Library

This branch of the Toronto Public Library has special sections devoted to children and can be traced to the 1922 founding of the Toronto's Boys and Girls House, the first library in the British Empire devoted exclusively to children. One of the branch's key collections is the Osborne Collection of Early Children's Books, which has more than eighty thousand items and includes gems such as Florence Nightingale's childhood library. The building itself is one of Toronto's strongest examples of the postmodern style.

There is little agreement about the dating of postmodernism, but it is generally thought of as emerging in the 1970s, reaching its zenith in the 1980s, and generally losing steam in the 1990s. This library, completed in 1995, is a late example of the style. Although postmodernism has endured a lot of contempt in recent years, the library, with its simple cubic volume, substantial materials, and integral ornament, is curiously satisfying.

Embedded in the classical tradition, the four-story building is massive, monolithic, and bilaterally symmetrical with a carefully articulated copper roof. Its facades, clad in pale-cream brick, are well-scaled, with two-story windows rising to a band of smaller windows on the third floor. A fourth-floor attic features diamond-brick patterning and tiny square windows. An elaborate, arched entry graces the College Street facade, accentuated by a pair of giant bronze griffins (guarding the library's treasures), and further marked above by a deep three-story cleft. Other pleasant aspects include a hefty, wood-clad service door on the east facade and a community garden at the rear.

127. Beverley Place (The Hydro Block), 15 Beverley Place and Nos. 6 through 28 Henry Street

A. J. Diamond & Barton Myers, 1976

In today's architectural parlance, this infill housing is referred to as a "fabric building" because it is carefully and quietly integrated into its dense urban context, unlike an "object building" that stands alone and shouts its presence. Beverley Place, which was realized by CityHome, a nonprofit housing company, has become a touchstone in Toronto for urban planners who believe high density can be achieved

Courtyard, Beverly Place

with low-rise construction just as well as or better than high-rise development. The project is also known as the Hydro Block because, originally, Ontario Hydro, the province's hydro-electric corporation, planned to construct a twelve-story transformer in the middle of the residential neighborhood—an area dominated by two- and three-story brick Victorian houses. Community activists stopped Ontario Hydro's blockbuster project, and architects Jack Diamond and Barton Myers were hired, having just completed the high-density, low-rise Sherbourne Lanes project on Toronto's east side.

Beverley Place consists of twelve preexisting houses and a new, five-floor U-shaped building faced in red-orange brick. Together, these form a large courtyard that contains both private backyards and a communal park.

The building section ingeniously combines town house and apartment unit types, which are revealed on the facades of the modernist building through the thoughtful and expressive location of doors and windows. Along the east side of the ramp down to the underground parking garage, Diamond and Myers, both of whom studied under architect Louis Kahn at the University of Pennsylvania, inserted three, huge circular openings, recalling Kahn's use of this geometric motif in many of his own projects.

128. Ontario College of Art and Design, 100 McCaul Street *Horwood & White, 1921*
Central building *Govan Ferguson Lindsay Kaminker Langley & Keenlyside, 1957*
South wing *Govan Ferguson Lindsay Kaminker Langley & Keenlyside, 1963*
North wing *Govan Kaminker Langley Keenlyside Melick Devonshire Wilson, 1967*
Sharp Centre for Design *Alsop Architects with Robbie Young + Wright, 2004*

Established in 1876 as the Ontario School of Art and incorporated as the Ontario College of Art in 1912, today's Ontario College of Art and Design (OCAD) is Canada's largest university of art and design. Its first building was designed by Horwood & White in close collaboration with the painter and, at the

Ontario College of Art and Design

time, principal of the college, George Reid. Completed in 1921 in the Georgian style, it was constructed on a site provided by the Art Gallery of Toronto (now the Art Gallery of Ontario). This original building remains at the northeast corner of Grange Park.

In recent years, OCAD has become a hothouse of innovation. The institution's newfound vitality was spurred by the 2004 construction of the Sharp Centre for Design, named for Isadore Sharp, founder of the Four Seasons Hotels chain, and his wife, OCAD alumna Rosalie Sharp. The building was designed by one of England's more outrageous architects, Will Alsop. When his "pixelated" box on stilts for OCAD was completed in 2004, it stirred tremendous controversy. But such a *tour de force* turned out to be the exact shock that OCAD needed to kick it into the twenty-first century; today the colorful building has settled into the greater urban environment while Torontonians move on to new architectural controversies.

The leggy pavilion recalls Archigram and Ron Herron's visionary project of 1964, "Walking City"—a dynamic city of components, networks, and grids, exuding youthful vitality. Alsop's elevated box is, in a 1960s sense, a happening. It feels as though it could start prancing across Grange Park to have a chat with the giant blue, titanium-clad box that Frank Gehry has perched atop the Art Gallery of Ontario—a sister volume that Gehry orchestrated with great care, urbanistically, to relate to and converse with Alsop's big black-and-white box.

129. Art Gallery of Ontario (AGO), 317 Dundas Street
West *Darling & Pearson, 1918, 1926*
Addition *Darling, Pearson & Cleveland, 1935*
Additions *John C. Parkin, 1974, 1977*
Additions and renovations *Barton Myers / Kuwabara Payne McKenna Blumberg Architects, 1993*
Additions and renovations *Gehry International Architects, 2008*

In 1910 Harriette Boulton Smith left her historic home, The Grange, and seven acres of property to the Art Museum of Toronto, which made most of the area available to the city as a public park. A year later, the prominent firm of Darling & Pearson was engaged to develop a design for a new museum to the north, to augment The Grange. Frank Darling generated a grand beaux arts scheme consisting of some thirty galleries organized around three interior courtyards, but by 1918 only a small fraction of the project had been built. A second phase, incorporating a sculpture court (Walker Court), was completed in 1926, and in 1935 Darling, Pearson & Cleveland added two more galleries.

The museum's collections and programs expanded dramatically over the next few decades, and major additions and renovations were undertaken in the mid-1970s and early 1990s, but by the mid-1990s it was clear that the Art Gallery of Ontario (AGO) once again lacked sufficient facilities and, equally important, architectural clarity. In the fall of 2002, with the promise of major gifts and support from Kenneth Thomson, a Canadian businessman and art collector, the AGO announced the appointment of Toronto-born Frank Owen Gehry as architect for its ambitious "Transformation AGO" project, which was brought to a conclusion six years later.

In this redesign of the AGO, Gehry made three bold moves: he recentered the main entrance on the historic Walker Court and bent this entrance axis vertically with a sculptural, upward-spiraling staircase; he added a six hundred-feet long, glass-skinned second-level sculpture promenade along Dundas Street; and he built an enormous blue-titanium-clad boxlike volume, housing contemporary galleries, above the historic Grange and overlooking Grange Park. Although the project has scores of other reworkings, it is these three moves that provided the underlying strategies allowing Gehry to spatially, sculpturally, and programmatically transform the institution. For Gehry, who grew up in the neighborhood surrounding the AGO, it was an intensely personal project. In the fall of 2005, he shared with me his first memory of the AGO, which he had visited as a child with his mother, Thelma Goldberg:

> It was my first time in an art museum. I think I was eight years old, and my mother took me. There was snow on the ground, and we were wearing galoshes. I remember a fence and a driveway and iron gates. The building was

Art Gallery of Ontario (during 2008 construction)

set back from the street, and you walked right into the Walker Court.... When the AGO hired me I saw right away that the circulation had become confusing. The original building had been added to piecemeal. My sense was, if we were going to redo the AGO, you could solve the confusion by centering the main entrance on the historic Walker Court.

Many aspects of Gehry's AGO design can be traced back to his early work in Los Angeles in the 1960s, 1970s, and early 1980s—projects such as Loyola Law School, MOCA's Temporary Contemporary, and Gehry's own residence in Santa Monica of 1978. These pre-Bilbao, pre–Walt Disney Concert Hall, less spectacular projects had a toughness and elemental quality that reappears in the AGO. Underlying zoomorphic preoccupations and interest in the primitive that have surfaced throughout Gehry's career are also present, from the fish-skeleton, ship-hull quality of the sculpture promenade along Dundas Street to the orgiastic stairs that curl up and down through the project. Moreover, Gehry's grand sense of history and time, along with his knowledge of and sensitivity to art, have brought to the AGO both new complexity and new clarity, making sense out of ninety years of architectural to and fro.

Acknowledgments

My deep interest in the architecture of the University of Toronto goes back to 1980, when I had just arrived as a young professor and been invited by the dean of the architecture school at the time, Blanche van Ginkel, to develop an introductory course on architecture for University College undergraduates. Teaching at the historic University College twenty-nine years ago triggered a desire to explore other buildings on the university's three campuses—something that I did from time to time, casually, over the next two decades. However, a structured, formal opportunity to fully study the university's buildings did not present itself until the spring of 2005 when the Princeton Architectural Press approached the university to discuss the possibility of creating a comprehensive campus guide (their first one about a campus outside the United States). I remain indebted to Kevin Lippert and Nancy Eklund Later at the press for first proposing that I write this guide and to key people at the university that attended the start-up meeting nearly four years ago and enthusiastically supported the book idea: Vivek Goel, vice-president and provost at the time; Ron Venter who was vice-provost, space and facilities planning; and Rivi Frankle, now chief operating officer and assistant vice-president, alumni relations. Two others participating in the 2005 meeting, Elizabeth Sisam, now assistant vice-president, campus and facilities planning, and George Baird, dean of the John H. Daniels Faculty of Architecture, Landscape, and Design, have provided valued encouragement, criticism, and support throughout the process, as has Professor Emeritus Martin Friedland, whose comprehensive knowledge of the history of the University of Toronto is without equal.

Conceptualizing, researching, writing, and illustrating a guide of this sort requires a team of people with a broad range of talent and skills. I was fortunate to bring Tom Arban on board as the photographer, and the pictures he produced are striking, to say the least. His careful documentation will serve as an important visual record of the university's buildings for decades to come. The book might never have gotten to the finish line without the assistance that I received from Robert Hill, an architect and meticulous researcher, who so generously shared his vast store of knowledge on Toronto architecture. Also, I am most grateful for the professionalism, patience, and precision of Nicola Bednarek, my editor at Princeton Architectural Press.

The John H. Daniels Faculty of Architecture, Landscape, and Design provided a collegial environment and crucial support. This included funding through the Ontario Work-Study Program for research assistance by undergraduates Bradley Chai and Ultan Byrne and graduate students Joel Legault, Mariangela Piccione, Luke Stern, Nancy-Ann Wilson, and Fan Zhang. Many faculty and staff members kindly assisted me in various ways; however, I must thank in particular Irene Puchalski, librarian of the Shore + Moffat Library, for arranging generous lending privileges, and Charles Cox, systems administrator, for rescuing me several times from an impending digital disaster. At the university level, I greatly appreciate the help that I received from Harold Averill, assistant university archivist, and Marnee Gamble, special media archivist, and others at the University of Toronto Archives at the Fisher Rare Book Library. Ian Orchard, vice-president and principal of the University of Toronto Mississauga, was very generous with his time, as was his colleague, Ray deSouza, chief administrative officer. Professor Edward (Ted) Relph was similarly kind in welcoming and assisting me at the University of Toronto Scarborough.

During the past four years, scores of people have, directly and indirectly, helped move the book along, and I wish I could list and thank every one of them. Trusting that I might be forgiven for imperfect recall, in addition to all those mentioned earlier I express my appreciation to John Buckley, Brent Cordner, Lisa Doherty, Maurice Farge, Adele Freedman, Matthew Gourlay, William Greer, Beth Hannah, Alan Hayes, Anna Lightfoot, Mary Louise Lobsinger, Mary Markou, Judy Matthews, John Bentley Mays, Janice Oliver, Stephen Otto, Stephen Phillips, Michelangelo Sabatino, Joseph Schner, Paolo Scrivano, Brigitte Shim, Geoffrey Simmins, Scott Sorli, and Mary Alice Thring. I am also grateful to Nene Brode, Ralph Burgess, Evelyn Collins, John P. M. Court, Anne Dale, Jim Derenzis, Don Dewees, Mike Filey, Mark Fram, Yvonne Hilder, Spencer Higgins, John Howarth, Evonne Levy, Yuri Lomakin, Dale Martin, Michael Marrus, Doug McBean, Anastasia Meletopoulos, Eha Naylor, George Phelphs, Sabina Pampor, Daniel Payne, Pina Petricone, Komala Prabhakar, David Rayside, Dennis Reid, Douglas Richardson, Kathryn Seymour, John Smegal, Graeme Stewart, Paul Stoesser, Kim Storey, Rudy Tyono, Alex Waugh, and Linda Wicks.

Throughout this privileged indulgence in the ideas behind and the architecture of some 170 buildings, I have been unfailingly supported by my partner of forty-two years, Frederic Urban, whose insights into history, architecture, and culture continue to propel me forward.

Larry Wayne Richards, Toronto, Canada

Bibliography

Collections and Files

Archives of Ontario
Campus and Facilities Planning, University of Toronto
City of Toronto Archives
City of Toronto Heritage Properties Inventory
Department of Facilities Management, University of Toronto Scarborough
Facilities and Services Department, University of Toronto
Ontario Heritage Trust
Real Estate Department and Capital Projects Department, University of Toronto
University of Toronto Archives, Fisher Rare Book Library
Utilities and Grounds Department, University of Toronto Mississauga

Books

Arthur, Eric. *From Front Street to Queen's Park*. Toronto: McClelland & Stewart, 1979.
Arthur, Eric. *Toronto No Mean City*. Toronto: University of Toronto Press, 1964.
Baraness, Marc and Larry Richards, eds. *Toronto Places: A Context for Urban Design*. Toronto: City of Toronto and University of Toronto Press, 1992.
Blackburn, Robert H. *Evolution of the Heart: A History of the University of Toronto Library Up To 1981*. Toronto: University of Toronto Press, 1987.
Blake, Samuel H. *Wycliffe College, An Historical Sketch*. Toronto: Wycliffe College, 1911.
Browne, Kelvin. *Bold Visions: The Architecture of the Royal Ontario Museum*. Toronto: Royal Ontario Museum, 2008.
Bureau of Architecture & Urbanism. *Toronto Modern: Architecture 1945–1965*. Toronto: Coach House Books and Association for Preservation Technology International, 2002.
Burwash, Nathaniel. *The History of Victoria College*. Toronto: The Victoria College Press, 1927.
Byrtus, Nancy, Mark Fram, and Michael McLelland, eds. *East/West: A Guide to Where People Live in Downtown Toronto*. Toronto: Coach House Press, 2000.
Carr, Angela. *Toronto Architect Edmund Burke: Redefining Canadian Architecture*. Montreal and Kingston: McGill-Queen's University Press, 1995.
Carter, Brian, ed. *Works: The Architecture of A. J. Diamond, Donald Schmitt and Company, 1968–1995*. Halifax: TUNS Press, 1996.

Dendy, William. *Lost Toronto*. Toronto: Oxford University Press, 1978.

Dendy, William and William Kilbourn. *Toronto Observed*: *Its Architecture, Patrons, and History*. Toronto: Oxford University Press, 1986.

Diamond, Jack, Don Gillmor, and Donald Schmitt. *Insight and On Site: The Architecture of Diamond and Schmitt*. Vancouver: Douglas & McIntyre, 2008.

Dobney, Stephen, ed. *Barton Myers: Selected and Current Works*. Victoria: The Images Publishing Group Pty Ltd, 1994.

Ede, Carol Moore. *Canadian Architecture 1960/70*. Toronto: Burns and MacEachern Limited, 1971.

Freedman, Adele. *Sight Lines: Looking at architecture and design in Canada*. Toronto: Oxford University Press, 1990.

Friedland, Martin L. *The University of Toronto: A History*. Toronto: University of Toronto Press, 2002.

Gournay, Isabelle. *Ernest Cormier and the Université de Montréal*. Montreal: Canadian Centre for Architecture, 1990.

Hart House: University of Toronto. Toronto: The Board of Governors, University of Toronto, 1921.

Kalman, Harold. *A History of Canadian Architecture* (Volumes 1 and 2). Toronto: Oxford University Press, 1994.

Kilgour, David, ed. *A Strange Elation: Hart House: The First Eighty Years*. Toronto: University of Toronto, 1999.

Kuwabara Payne McKenna Blumberg. Gloucester, Massachusetts: Rockport Publishers, 1998.

Litvak, Marilyn M. *Edward James Lennox, "Builder of Toronto."* Toronto: Dundurn Press, 1995.

Mays, John Bentley. *Emerald City: Toronto Visited*. Toronto: Viking, 1994.

Martyn, Lucy B. *The Face of Early Toronto: An Archival Record, 1797–1936*. Ontario: Sutton West / Paget Press, 1982.

McClelland, Michael and Graeme Stewart, eds. *Concrete Toronto: A Guidebook to Concrete Architecture from the Fifties to the Seventies*. Toronto: Coach House Press and E.R.A. Architects, 2007.

McHugh, Patricia. *Toronto Architecture: A City Guide*. Toronto: Mercury Books, 1985.

Reed, T. A. *The History of Trinity College, 1852–1952*. Toronto: The University of Toronto Press, 1952.

Reid, Dennis, ed. *Frank Gehry: Toronto*. Toronto: The Art Gallery of Ontario, 2006.

Richardson, Douglas. *A Not Unsightly Building: University College and Its History*. Oakville, Ontario: Mosaic Press, 1990.

Rickets, Shannon, Leslie Maitland, and Jacqueline Hucker. *A Guide to Canadian Architectural Styles*. Peterborough, Ontario: Broadview Press, 2004.

Rochon, Lisa. *Up North: Where Canada's Architecture Meets the Land*. Toronto:

Key Porter Books, 2005.

Simmins, Geoffrey. *Fred Cumberland: Building the Victorian Dream*. Toronto: University of Toronto Press, 1997.

Simmins, Geoffrey. *Ontario Association of Architects: A Centennial History, 1889–1989*. Toronto: Ontario Association of Architects, 1989.

Stanwick, Sean and J. Flores. *Design City Toronto*. Chicester, West Sussex, England: John Wiley & Sons Ltd., 2007.

The Architecture of Kuwabara Payne McKenna Blumberg. Basel: Birkhauser Ltd., 2004.

Westfall, William. *The Founding Moment: Church, Society, and the Construction of Trinity College*. Montreal and Kingston: McGill-Queen's University Press, 2002.

White, Richard. *The Skule Story: The University of Toronto Faculty of Applied Science and Engineering, 1873–2000*. Toronto: Faculty of Applied Science and Engineering, University of Toronto, 2000.

Booklets, Guides, Reports, and Selected Articles

"A Brief Guide to Massey College." Toronto: Massey College, June 1994.

A.D. Margison and Associates Limited. *University of Toronto: Interim Report for the Complete Design and Supervision of Construction of Buildings and Site Development for the Erindale Campus*. April 5, 1967.

A.D. Margison and Associates Limited with Raymond Moriyama, Planning and Architectural Consultant. *University of Toronto: Master Plan: Report on Phasing and Planning for the Erindale Campus*. Issue Numbers I and II, Summer 1967.

A.D. Margison and Associates Limited. *University of Toronto: Master Plan Report on Phasing and Planning for the Erindale Campus*. Issue Number III, Volume I (December 1972) and Volume II (May 1972).

Andrews, John, Michael Hough, Donovan Pinker, and Evan Walker. *Erindale Campus Master Plan, University of Toronto*. December 1966.

Bissell, Claude. "University of Toronto Expansion Program – A Reflection of Academic Policy and Ideals." *The Journal of The Royal Architectural Institute of Canada*. xxxvii, January 1960, 6–10.

Black, J. Bernard. *Familiar Landmarks: Four Walks Through the Historic Campus of the University of St. Michael's College*. Toronto: University of St. Michael's College, 1984.

Chapman, Howard. "The Campus Development Plan." *The Journal of The Royal Architectural Institute of Canada*, xxxvii, January 1960, 24–26.

Fleming, Bryant, *A Report Accompanying A Preliminary Plan for the Landscape Improvement and General Expansion for the University of Toronto, Toronto,*

Ont. Buffalo, New York, November 1917.

Greer, William. "Trinity College Quadrangle." Report for the Trinity College Provost's Quadrangle Committee, January 2006.

Office of the Assistant Vice-President (Planning). *University of Toronto Campus Master Plan (Discussion Draft).* University of Toronto, 1991.

Office of Convocation. *Trinity College: A Walking Guide.* University of Trinity College, University of Toronto, 2001.

Percy, John and Sabeen Abbas, eds. *Celebrating 40 Years of History at the University of Toronto Mississauga.* Toronto: U of T Mississauga, 2007.

Richards, Larry W. and Craig Handy. *A Report on the Education Centre Architecture and Art,* April 2004.

Seymour, Kathryn. *An Architectural-Historical Report on The Koffler Scientific Reserve at Joker's Hill.* Commissioned by the University of Toronto, June 2004.

Students' Administrative Council. *The Campus as the Campus Centre: A Manual.* Toronto: Students' Administrative Council, University of Toronto, 1971.

The New Woodsworth College. Woodsworth College, 1994.

Urban Strategies Ltd. *Investing in the Landscape* (Open Space Master Plan). Toronto, 1999.

Wright, C.H.C. "University of Toronto." *The Journal of The Royal Architectural Institute of Canada.* ii, January–March 1925, 2–23.

Illustration Credits

Index

(Italics indicate a photograph. The letter "m" indicates a map.)